PRACTICE – ASSESS – DIAGNOSE

180 Days of LANGUAGE
for Second Grade

hop

- ✔ capitalization
- ✔ punctuation
- ✔ parts of speech
- ✔ spelling

Author
Christine Dugan, M.A.Ed.

Shell Education

Image Credits

All images Shutterstock

Standards

© Copyright 2010. National Governors Association Center for Best Practices and Council of Chief State School Officers. All rights reserved.

Shell Education
5482 Argosy Avenue
Huntington Beach, CA 92649-1030
www.tcmpub.com/shell-education
ISBN 978-1-4258-1167-9
© 2020 Shell Education Publishing, Inc.

TABLE OF CONTENTS

Introduction and Research............................... 3

How to Use This Book................................... 5

Standards Correlations 11

Daily Practice Pages 12

Answer Key 192

References Cited......................................207

Digital Resources 208

INTRODUCTION AND RESEARCH

People who love the English language often lament the loss of grammar knowledge and the disappearance of systematic grammar instruction. We wince at emails with errors, such as when the noun *advice is* used instead of the verb *advise*. We may set aside a résumé with the incorrect placement of an apostrophe. And some of us pore (not pour) over entertaining punctuation guides such as *Eats, Shoots and Leaves* by Lynne Truss (2003). We chuckle over collections of bloopers such as *Anguished English: An Anthology of Accidental Assaults upon Our Language* by Richard Lederer (1987).

Even though we worry about grammar, our students arrive at school with a complex set of grammar rules in place—albeit affected by the prevailing dialect (Hillocks and Smith 2003, 727). For example, while students may not be able to recite the rule for where to position an adjective, they know intuitively to say *the yellow flower* instead of *the flower yellow*. All this knowledge comes without formal instruction. Further, young people easily shift between articulating or writing traditional patterns of grammar and communicating complete sentences with startling efficiency: IDK (I don't know), and for the ultimate in brevity, K (okay).

So, if students speak fairly well and have already mastered a complex written shorthand, why study grammar? Researchers provide us with three sound reasons:

1. the insights it offers into the way the language works

2. its usefulness in mastering standard forms of English

3. its usefulness in improving composition skills (Hillocks and Smith 1991, 594)

INTRODUCTION AND RESEARCH *(cont.)*

Studying grammar also provides users—teachers, students, and parents—with a common vocabulary to discuss both spoken and written language. The Assembly for the Teaching of English Grammar states, "Grammar is important because it is the language that makes it possible for us to talk about language. Grammar names the types of words and word groups that make up sentences not only in English but in any language. As human beings, we can put sentences together even as children—we all *do* grammar. But to be able to talk about how sentences are built, about the types of words and word groups that make up sentences—that is *knowing about* grammar."

With the publication of the college and career readiness standards, key instructional skills are identified, such as identifying parts of speech, using prepositional phrases, capitalizing, and correctly using commas. Writing conventions such as punctuation serve an important function for the reader—setting off syntactic units and providing intonational cues and semantic information. Capitalization provides the reader with such cues as sentence beginnings and proper nouns (Hodges 1991, 779).

The Need for Practice

To be successful in today's classroom, students must deeply understand both concepts and procedures so that they can discuss and demonstrate their understanding. Demonstrating understanding is a process that must be continually practiced in order for students to be successful. According to Marzano, "practice has always been, and always will be, a necessary ingredient to learning procedural knowledge at a level at which students execute it independently" (2010, 83). Practice is especially important to help students apply their concrete, conceptual understanding of a particular language skill.

Understanding Assessment

In addition to providing opportunities for frequent practice, teachers must be able to assess students' comprehension and word-study skills. This is important so that teachers can adequately address students' misconceptions, build on their current understanding, and challenge them appropriately. Assessment is a long-term process that often involves careful analysis of student responses from a lesson discussion, project, practice sheet, or test. When analyzing the data, it is important for teachers to reflect on how their teaching practices may have influenced students' responses, and to identify those areas where additional instruction may be required. In short, the data gathered from assessments should be used to inform instruction: slow down, speed up, or reteach. This type of assessment is called *formative assessment*.

HOW TO USE THIS BOOK

With *180 Days of Language,* students receive practice with punctuation, identifying parts of speech, capitalization, and spelling. The daily practice will develop students' writing efforts and oral reading skills.

Easy to Use and Standards-Based

These activities reinforce grade-level skills across a variety of language concepts. The questions are provided as a full practice page, making them easy to prepare and implement as part of a classroom morning routine, at the beginning of each language arts lesson, or as homework.

Every practice page provides questions that are tied to a language standard. Students are given opportunities for regular practice in language skills, allowing them to build confidence through these quick standards-based activities.

Question	Language Skill	College and Career Readiness Standard
1	capitalization	**Language Standard 2.2a**—Capitalize holidays, product names, and geographic names.
2–3	punctuation	**Language Standard 2.2b**—Use commas in greetings and closings of letters. **Language Standard 2.2c**—Use an apostrophe to form contractions and frequently occurring possessives.
4–5	parts of speech	**Language Standard 2.1a**—Use collective nouns. **Language Standard 2.1b**—Form and use frequently occurring irregular plural nouns. **Language Standard 2.1c**—Use reflexive pronouns. **Language Standard 2.1d**—Form and use the past tense of frequently occurring irregular verbs. **Language Standard 2.1e**— Use adjectives and adverbs, and choose between them depending on what is to be modified.
6	spelling	**Language Standard 2.2d**—Generalize learned spelling patterns when writing words.

Note: Because articles and possessive pronouns are also adjectives, they are included in the answer key as such. Depending on students knowledge of this, grade activity sheets accordingly.

HOW TO USE THIS BOOK *(cont.)*

Using the Practice Pages

Practice pages provide instruction and assessment opportunities for each day of the school year. Teachers may wish to prepare packets of weekly practice pages for the classroom or for homework. As outlined on page 5, every question is aligned to a language skill.

Practice pages provide instruction and assessment opportunities for each day of the school year.

Each question ties student practice to a specific language skill.

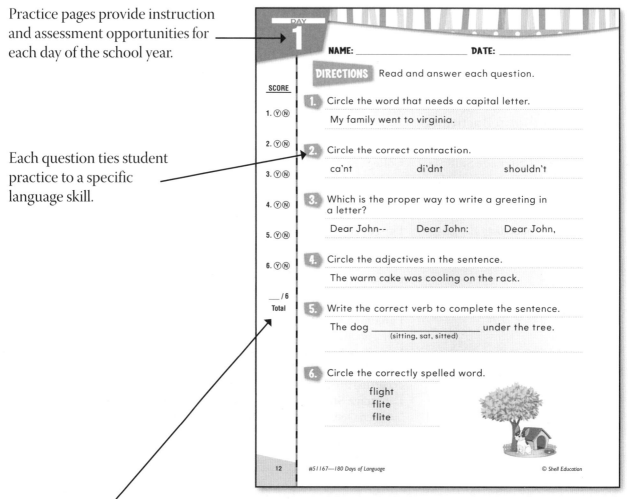

DAY 1

NAME: _____ DATE: _____

DIRECTIONS Read and answer each question.

SCORE

1. Ⓨ Ⓝ

2. Ⓨ Ⓝ

3. Ⓨ Ⓝ

4. Ⓨ Ⓝ

5. Ⓨ Ⓝ

6. Ⓨ Ⓝ

___/ 6
Total

1. Circle the word that needs a capital letter.

My family went to virginia.

2. Circle the correct contraction.

ca'nt   di'dnt   shouldn't

3. Which is the proper way to write a greeting in a letter?

Dear John--   Dear John: Dear John,

4. Circle the adjectives in the sentence.

The warm cake was cooling on the rack.

5. Write the correct verb to complete the sentence.

The dog _____ under the tree.
(sitting, sat, sitted)

6. Circle the correctly spelled word.

flight
flite
flite

12   #51167—180 Days of Language   © Shell Education

Using the Scoring Guide

Use the scoring guide along the side of each practice page to check answers and see at a glance which skills may need more reinforcement.

Fill in the appropriate circle for each problem to indicate correct (Y) or incorrect (N) responses. You might wish to indicate only incorrect responses to focus on those skills. (For example, if students consistently miss items 2 and 4, they may need additional help with those concepts as outlined in the table on page 5.) Use the answer key at the back of the book to score the problems, or you may call out answers to have students self-score or peer-score their work.

HOW TO USE THIS BOOK (cont.)

Diagnostic Assessment

Teachers can use the practice pages as diagnostic assessments. The data analysis tools included with the book enable teachers or parents to quickly score students' work and monitor their progress. Teachers and parents can see at a glance which language skills students may need to target in order to develop proficiency.

After students complete a practice page, grade each page using the answer key (pages 192–206). Then, complete the *Practice Page Item Analysis* for the appropriate day (page 8) for the whole class, or the *Student Item Analysis* (page 9) for individual students. These charts are also provided in the digital resources (filenames: G2_practicepage_analysis.pdf, G2_student_analysis.pdf). Teachers can input data into the electronic files directly on the computer, or they can print the pages and analyze students' work using paper and pencil.

To complete the Practice Page Item Analyses:

- Write or type students' names in the far-left column. Depending on the number of students, more than one copy of the form may be needed, or you may need to add rows.

- The item numbers are included across the top of the chart. Each item correlates with the matching question number from the practice page.

- For each student, record an *X* in the column if the student has the item incorrect. If the item is correct, leave the space in the column blank.

- Count the *X*s in each row and column and fill in the correct boxes.

To complete the Student Item Analyses:

- Write or type the student's name on the top row. This form tracks the ongoing progress of each student, so one copy per student is necessary.

- The item numbers are included across the top of the chart. Each item correlates with the matching question number from the practice page.

- For each day, record an *X* in the column if the student has the item incorrect. If the item is correct, leave the space in the column blank.

- Count the *X*s in each row and column and fill in the correct boxes.

Practice Page Item Analysis

Directions: Record an X in cells to indicate where students have missed questions. Add up the totals. You can view: (1) which questions/concepts were missed per student; (2) the total correct score for each student; and (3) the total number of students who missed each question.

Day: _____ Question # Student Name	1	2	3	4	5	6	# correct
Sample Student		x			x	x	3/6
# of students missing each question							

HOW TO USE THIS BOOK *(cont.)*

Student Item Analysis

Directions: Record an *X* in cells to indicate where the student has missed questions. Add up the totals. You can view: (1) which questions/concepts the student missed; (2) the total correct score per day; and (3) the total number of times each question/concept was missed.

Student Name: **Sample Student**							
Question	1	2	3	4	5	6	# correct
Day							
1		X			X		4/6
Total							

HOW TO USE THIS BOOK *(cont.)*

Using the Results to Differentiate Instruction

Once results are gathered and analyzed, teachers can use the results to inform the way they differentiate instruction. The data can help determine which concepts are the most difficult for students and which need additional instructional support and continued practice. Depending on how often the practice pages are scored, results can be considered for instructional support on a daily or weekly basis.

Whole-Class Support

The results of the diagnostic analysis may show that the entire class is struggling with a particular concept or group of concepts. If these concepts have been taught in the past, this indicates that further instruction or reteaching is necessary. If these concepts have not been taught in the past, this data is a great preassessment and may demonstrate that students do not have a working knowledge of the concepts. Thus, careful planning for the length of the unit(s) or lesson(s) must be considered, and additional front-loading may be required.

Small-Group or Individual Support

The results of the diagnostic analysis may show that an individual or a small group of students is struggling with a particular concept or group of concepts. If these concepts have been taught in the past, this indicates that further instruction or reteaching is necessary. Consider pulling aside these students while others are working independently to instruct further on the concept(s). Teachers can also use the results to help identify individuals or groups of proficient students who are ready for enrichment or above-grade-level instruction. These students may benefit from independent learning contracts or more challenging activities. Students may also benefit from extra practice using games or computer-based resources.

Digital Resources

Reference page 208 for information about accessing the digital resources and an overview of the contents.

STANDARDS CORRELATIONS

Shell Education is committed to producing educational materials that are research and standards based. All products are correlated to the academic standards of all 50 states, the District of Columbia, the Department of Defense Dependent Schools, and the Canadian provinces.

How to Find Standards Correlations

To print a customized correlation report of this product for your state, visit **www.tcmpub.com/ administrators/correlations/** and follow the online directions. If you require assistance in printing correlation reports, please contact the Customer Service Department at 1-877-777-3450.

Purpose and Intent of Standards

The Every Student Succeeds Act (ESSA) mandates that all states adopt challenging academic standards that help students meet the goal of college and career readiness. While many states already adopted academic standards prior to ESSA, the act continues to hold states accountable for detailed and comprehensive standards.

Standards are designed to focus instruction and guide adoption of curricula. Standards are statements that describe the criteria necessary for students to meet specific academic goals. They define the knowledge, skills, and content students should acquire at each level. Standards are also used to develop standardized tests to evaluate students' academic progress. Teachers are required to demonstrate how their lessons meet state standards. State standards are used in the development of all Shell products, so educators can be assured they meet the academic requirements of each state.

College and Career Readiness

In this book, the following college and career readiness (CCR) standard is met: Spell grade-appropriate words correctly, consulting references as needed.

McREL Compendium

Each year, McREL analyzes state standards and revises the compendium to produce a general compilation of national standards. In this book, the following standards are met: Demonstrate command of the conventions of standard English capitalization, punctuation, and spelling when writing; spell grade-appropriate words correctly, consulting references as needed.

TESOL and WIDA Standards

In this book, the following English language development standards are met: Standard 1: English language learners communicate for social and instructional purposes within the school setting. Standard 2: English language learners communicate information, ideas, and concepts necessary for academic success in the content area of language arts.

NAME: _____ **DATE:** _____

SCORE

DIRECTIONS Read and answer each question.

1. (Y) (N)

1. Circle the word that needs a capital letter.

My family went to virginia.

2. (Y) (N)

2. Circle the correct contraction.

ca'nt   di'dnt   shouldn't

3. (Y) (N)

3. Which is the proper way to write a greeting in a letter?

4. (Y) (N)

Dear John--   Dear John: Dear John,

5. (Y) (N)

4. Circle the adjectives in the sentence.

The warm cake was cooling on the rack.

6. (Y) (N)

___ / 6
Total

5. Write the correct verb to complete the sentence.

The dog _____ under the tree.
            (sitting, sat, sitted)

6. Circle the correctly spelled word.

flight
flite
flite

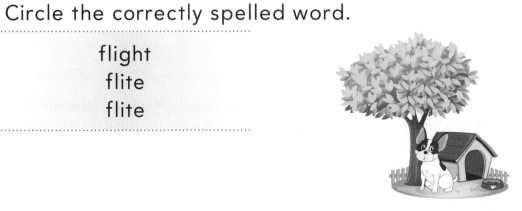

NAME: _____ **DATE:** _____

DIRECTIONS Read and answer each question.

1. Which word is always capitalized?

Christmas   A   Love

1. Ⓨ Ⓝ

2. Circle the correct contraction.

willn't   won't   wo'nt

2. Ⓨ Ⓝ

3. Ⓨ Ⓝ

3. How would you sign a letter to a family member?

Love,   Love   Love.

4. Ⓨ Ⓝ

4. What is the plural of *tooth*?

tooths   toothes   teeth

5. Ⓨ Ⓝ

6. Ⓨ Ⓝ

5. Circle the adverb in the sentence.

The car sped quickly to the train station.

___ / 6
Total

6. Circle the word that is spelled correctly.

taugh   tawt   taught

NAME: _____ **DATE:** _____

DIRECTIONS Read and answer each question.

1. Circle the words that need capital letters.

The san francisco map showed me where to go.

2. Circle the correct contraction.

weren't   wev'e   its'

3. Which letter greeting uses the correct punctuation?

Dearest Lily,   Dearest, Lily   Dearest Lily.

4. Which pair of words includes the correct singular and plural tenses?

foot/foots   child/children   fish/fishs

5. Write the correct pronoun.

The kids are not allowed to help _____ to dessert.
(them, they, themselves)

6. Circle the word that is spelled correctly.

squair   square   sqware

#51167—180 Days of Language

NAME: _____ **DATE:** _____

DIRECTIONS Read and answer each question.

1. Write the name of your school with correct capitalization.

_____

1. Ⓨ Ⓝ

2. What is another way to write *a bone belonging to a dog*?

a dogs bone   a dog's bone   a dogs' bone

2. Ⓨ Ⓝ

3. Ⓨ Ⓝ

3. What always comes after the word *Sincerely* in a letter's closing?

,   :   ;

4. Ⓨ Ⓝ

5. Ⓨ Ⓝ

4. Write an adjective to complete the sentence.

The _____ dog was chasing a squirrel.

6. Ⓨ Ⓝ

5. What is the plural of *man*?

man's   mans   men

___ / 6
Total

6. Circle the correctly spelled word.

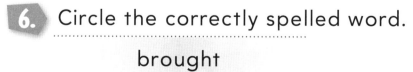

brought
brot
brawt

NAME: _____ **DATE:** _____

DIRECTIONS Read and answer each question.

1. Write the name of where you live using correct capitalization.

_____

2. What is another way to write *the party of a friend*?

a friend's party   a friends party   a friend,s party

3. How might you close a letter to your friend?

Your friend   Your friend,   Your friend…

4. Circle the adverb in the sentence.

The turtle moved slowly along the path.

5. Which is the correct plural word?

sheep   sheeps   sheepes

6. Circle the correctly spelled word.

fixture
fixter
fixtcher

 #51167—*180 Days of Language*

NAME: _____ **DATE:** _____

DIRECTIONS Read and answer each question.

1. Circle the word in the sentence that should **not** start with a capital letter.

1. Ⓨ Ⓝ

The King Deli has a special Menu on Halloween.

2. Ⓨ Ⓝ

2. Place the comma in the proper place for a letter greeting.

3. Ⓨ Ⓝ

Dear Nana

4. Ⓨ Ⓝ

3. Which is the proper way to write *the cake belongs to Frank*?

5. Ⓨ Ⓝ

Franks cake   Frank's cake   Franks' cake

6. Ⓨ Ⓝ

4. Write the correct word to complete the sentence.

The _____ of birds filled the sky.
    (pack, team, flock)

___/ 6
Total

5. Write the correct adjective to complete the sentence.

I was not sure what to draw on the _____
paper.   (blank, delicious, salty)

6. Circle the word that is spelled correctly.

clewn   clown   cloun

NAME: _____ DATE: _____

DIRECTIONS Read and answer each question.

1. (Y)(N)

2. (Y)(N)

3. (Y)(N)

4. (Y)(N)

5. (Y)(N)

6. (Y)(N)

___ / 6
Total

1. Which word is always capitalized?

Birthday   Stop   California

2. Place the comma in the proper place for a letter closing.

Love Sydney

3. Circle the correct contraction.

I'ts   I'm   Iv'e

4. What word describes a group of flowers?

pack   bouquet   team

5. Circle the adverb in the sentence.

I need to move my hand carefully while I paint.

6. Circle the correctly spelled word.

slow
slooe
slouw

NAME: _____ **DATE:** _____

DIRECTIONS   Read and answer each question.

1.   Circle the words that need capital letters.

Where can I find the main street library?

2.   Write a greeting for the letter.

_____

Thank you for my birthday present. I loved it very much. I'm so glad that you came to my party.

3.   Circle the correct contraction.

are'nt   arn't   aren't

4.   Circle the adjectives in the sentence.

My dad's fancy car goes fast down the street.

5.   Write the correct word to complete the sentence.

Let's play with a _____ of cards.

(bowl, range, deck)

6.   Circle the word that is spelled correctly.

needet   neded   needed

1. Ⓨ Ⓝ

2. Ⓨ Ⓝ

3. Ⓨ Ⓝ

4. Ⓨ Ⓝ

5. Ⓨ Ⓝ

6. Ⓨ Ⓝ

___ / 6
Total

NAME: _____ DATE: _____

DIRECTIONS Read and answer each question.

1. (Y)(N)

1. Write the name of your favorite holiday with correct capitalization.

_____

2. (Y)(N)

2. What is another way to write *the book belonging to my teacher*?

| my teachers book | my teachers' book | my teacher's book |

3. (Y)(N)

3. What always comes after the word *Love* in a letter closing?

,   :   ;

4. (Y)(N)

4. Write an adjective to complete the sentence.

The _____ girl took candy away from her brother.

5. (Y)(N)

5. Write a noun to complete the sentence.

I can see a stack of _____ in my house.

6. (Y)(N)

6. Circle the word that is spelled correctly.

each   eche   eatch

___/6
Total

NAME: _____   DATE: _____

DIRECTIONS Read and answer each question.

1. Circle the words that need capital letters.

My favorite brand of granola bars is natural bars.

2. Add an apostrophe to the sentence.

The artists work is very special to him.

3. How would you close a letter to a teacher?

Your student   Your student,   Your student...

4. What is the past tense of *begin*?

begined   beginning   began

5. What would you call a group of soldiers?

an army   a tribe   a class

6. Circle the corrrectly spelled word.

bothe
bolth
both

NAME: _____ DATE: _____

DIRECTIONS Read and answer each question.

1. Circle the word that needs a capital letter.

The islands in hawaii are beautiful!

2. Write a greeting that you would write in a letter to your teacher.

_____

3. Rewrite the sentence with a contraction.

The bus driver will not pick up kids who are late.

_____

_____

4. Circle the adjectives in the sentence.

My party took place on a hot day.

5. What is the past tense of *have*?

haved   havt   had

6. Circle the word that has an *-ow* spelling pattern that sounds the same in *clown*.

low   tow   cow

NAME: _____ **DATE:** _____

DIRECTIONS Read and answer each question.

1. Circle the word that needs a capital letter.

The store sells apple® computers.

1. Ⓨ Ⓝ

2. Which contraction means "cannot"?

cann't   ca'nt   can't

2. Ⓨ Ⓝ

3. Ⓨ Ⓝ

3. Use an apostrophe to write *the cub that belongs to the tiger* in another way.

_____

4. Ⓨ Ⓝ

5. Ⓨ Ⓝ

4. Which shows a correct singular and plural?

one car/   one table/   one cat/
two cars   two table   two cat

6. Ⓨ Ⓝ

5. Write the correct adverb to complete the sentence.

My friend _____ said yes to the
invitation.   (gladly, happy)

___ / 6
Total

6. Circle the word that has an *-oa* spelling pattern that sounds the same in *road*.

soar
coat
boar

NAME: _____ DATE: _____

SCORE

DIRECTIONS Read and answer each question.

1. Ⓨ Ⓝ

2. Ⓨ Ⓝ

3. Ⓨ Ⓝ

4. Ⓨ Ⓝ

5. Ⓨ Ⓝ

6. Ⓨ Ⓝ

___ / 6
Total

1. Write a sentence about what you ate for breakfast with correct capitalization.

_____

_____

2. Circle the contraction in the sentence.

You can't pick flowers from a person's garden!

3. Write a greeting for a letter to your best friend.

_____

4. What would you call a large number of flowers?

a group of flowers   a bouquet of flowers   a herd of flowers

5. Write the correct pronoun to complete the sentence.

The students can locate their book bags

_____.

(them, they, themselves)

6. Circle the word that is spelled correctly.

watsh   wach   watch

NAME: _____ **DATE:** _____

DIRECTIONS   Read and answer each question.

1. Which word is always capitalized?

| Name | Car | Canada |

2. Use an apostrophe to write *the hair on Phoebe* in another way.

_____

3. Add commas to the letter.

Dear Finn
Will you come to my house? My mom says that Monday is a good day.
Your friend
Jesse

4. Write an adjective to complete the sentence.

The _____ plant was the prettiest in the garden.

5. Write the correct plural word in the blank.

A large group of _____ toured the building.
(man, mans, men)

6. Circle the word that is spelled correctly.

| fence | fens | fense |

NAME: _____   DATE: _____

DIRECTIONS   Read and answer each question.

SCORE

1. Ⓨ Ⓝ

2. Ⓨ Ⓝ

3. Ⓨ Ⓝ

4. Ⓨ Ⓝ

5. Ⓨ Ⓝ

6. Ⓨ Ⓝ

___ / 6
Total

1. Circle the word that needs a capital letter.

Do you celebrate christmas or a different holiday?

2. Add apostrophes to the sentence.

I dont want to go to Patricks party.

3. Add apostrophes to the following contractions.

wont   didnt   shouldnt

4. Circle the adverb in the sentence.

Jose's grandmother asked him to ride his
bike safely.

5. Circle the plural word in the sentence.

Six children were in a group on the field trip.

6. Circle the correctly spelled word.

flow
flo
floa

NAME: _____ **DATE:** _____

DIRECTIONS Read and answer each question.

1. Circle the words that need capital letters.

Have you heard of the great barrier reef?

1. Ⓨ Ⓝ

2. How would you address a letter to your local newspaper?

_____

2. Ⓨ Ⓝ

3. Ⓨ Ⓝ

3. Rewrite the sentence with a contraction.

I cannot turn in my homework today.

_____

_____

4. Ⓨ Ⓝ

5. Ⓨ Ⓝ

6. Ⓨ Ⓝ

4. Circle the adjectives in the sentence.

The blue fish swam through the clear water.

___ / 6
Total

5. Write the plural noun to complete the sentence.

The _____ boarded the bus in the morning.
(person)

6. Circle the two words that have -*ai* spelling patterns and sound the same.

mail   said   main

NAME: _____ **DATE:** _____

SCORE

1. Ⓨ Ⓝ

2. Ⓨ Ⓝ

3. Ⓨ Ⓝ

4. Ⓨ Ⓝ

5. Ⓨ Ⓝ

6. Ⓨ Ⓝ

___ / 6
Total

DIRECTIONS Read and answer each question.

1. Circle the word that needs a capital letter.

The directions told me how to update my microsoft® software.

2. Circle the correct contraction.

Ih've   Iv'e   I've

3. Use an apostrophe to write *the coat that belongs to Lily* in another way.

_____

4. Many plural nouns end in *-s* or *-es*. Which noun does **not** follow this rule?

toe   foot   finger

5. Circle the adverb in the sentence.

The tiger happily ate its lunch in the sun.

6. Circle the two words that have *-ea* spelling patterns that sound the same.

sea
bread
beach

NAME: _____ **DATE:** _____

DIRECTIONS Read and answer each question.

1. Write a sentence about your favorite restaurant with correct capitalization.

_____

_____

1. Ⓨ Ⓝ

2. Ⓨ Ⓝ

2. Circle the contraction in the sentence.

Soccer wasn't always my favorite sport.

3. Ⓨ Ⓝ

3. Write a greeting for a letter to a family member.

_____

4. Ⓨ Ⓝ

4. What would you call a large amount of ants?

an army of ants   a herd of ants   a flock of ants

5. Ⓨ Ⓝ

6. Ⓨ Ⓝ

5. Circle the pronoun in the sentence.

Kiana is going to treat herself to a frozen yogurt after the big game.

___ / 6
Total

6. Circle the correctly spelled word.

toe

towe

toew

NAME: _____ **DATE:** _____

DIRECTIONS Read and answer each question.

1. Which word is always capitalized?

Florida   The   A

2. Use an apostrophe to write *the book from my teacher* in another way.

_____

3. Add commas to the letter.

Dear Maya
I hope you have a great birthday.
Your friend
Maria

4. Write an adjective to complete the sentence.

The _____ spider wove a web on the tree branch.

5. Write a sentence using the word *pair* to describe two objects.

_____

_____

6. Circle the word that is spelled correctly.

neat   neet   neatt

  #51167—180 Days of Language

NAME: _____ **DATE:** _____

DIRECTIONS Read and answer each question.

1. What types of words are always capitalized?

holiday names   contractions   adverbs

2. Add apostrophes to the sentence.

I shouldnt have to pick up Juans clothes because that is his job!

3. Add apostrophes to the following contractions.

cant   mustnt   weve

4. Circle the adverb in the sentence.

The field trip went terribly since we missed our bus.

5. Write a noun in the blank that makes sense.

There were six animals in the litter of

_____.

6. Circle the word that is spelled correctly.

blu   bluw   blue

1. Ⓨ Ⓝ

2. Ⓨ Ⓝ

3. Ⓨ Ⓝ

4. Ⓨ Ⓝ

5. Ⓨ Ⓝ

6. Ⓨ Ⓝ

___ / 6
Total

NAME: _____ **DATE:** _____

SCORE

1. Ⓨ Ⓝ

2. Ⓨ Ⓝ

3. Ⓨ Ⓝ

4. Ⓨ Ⓝ

5. Ⓨ Ⓝ

6. Ⓨ Ⓝ

___/6
Total

DIRECTIONS Read and answer each question.

1. Write a sentence about a special place that you would like to visit using correct capitalization.

_____

_____

2. Add punctuation to the letter greeting.

Dear Mr Franklin

3. Circle the contraction in the sentence.

The police officer should've pulled over that car for speeding.

4. Write an adjective to complete the sentence.

The _____ book was very scary because it seems real!

5. What is the past tense of the word *buy*?

buying   buyed   bought

6. Circle the word that is spelled correctly.

chanj   chanje   change

NAME: _____ **DATE:** _____

DIRECTIONS Read and answer each question.

1. Circle the word that needs a capital letter.

I like to use crayola® markers.

1. Ⓨ Ⓝ

2. Circle the correct contraction.

could've   couldh'of   could'hve

2. Ⓨ Ⓝ

3. Ⓨ Ⓝ

3. Use an apostrophe to write *the pair of shoes that belong to Veronica* in another way.

_____

4. Ⓨ Ⓝ

4. Write an adverb to complete the sentence.

The sea turtle waddled _____ to cross the beach.

5. Ⓨ Ⓝ

6. Ⓨ Ⓝ

5. Circle the adjectives in the sentence.

The strong coffee was served in a mug.

___ / 6
Total

6. Circle the correctly spelled word.

cince
scince
since

NAME: _____ **DATE:** _____

1. Y N

2. Y N

3. Y N

4. Y N

5. Y N

6. Y N

___ / 6
Total

DIRECTIONS Read and answer each question.

1. Write the brand name of a product in your home.

_____

2. Add a contraction to the sentence.

Why _____ we take a ball out for recess?
(cannot)

3. Add commas to the letter.

Dear Editor
I think we need more parks. They are important
for our health.
Sincerely
Luis

4. What would you call a group of islands?

chain of
islands

herd of
islands

flock of
islands

5. Write the correct pronoun to complete the sentence.

Tasha is able to finish her homework

_____.
(yourself, herself)

6. Circle the word that is spelled correctly.

dans   dance   danse

NAME: _____ **DATE:** _____

DIRECTIONS Read and answer each question.

1. Which word is always capitalized?

Vacation   Hawaii   Airplane

1. Ⓨ Ⓝ

2. What is another way to write *the pizza from the restaurant*?

| the restaurants' pizza | the restauran'ts pizza | the restaurant's pizza |

2. Ⓨ Ⓝ

3. Ⓨ Ⓝ

3. Add commas to the letter.

Dear Mom
You are the best mom ever. Thank you for the new video game.
Love
Joey

4. Ⓨ Ⓝ

5. Ⓨ Ⓝ

6. Ⓨ Ⓝ

___ / 6
Total

4. Circle the adverb in the sentence.

The car moved slowly through the parking lot.

5. What is the past tense of the word *shake*?

shaked   shooken   shook

6. Circle the word that is spelled correctly.

citty   city   sity

NAME: _____ DATE: _____

DIRECTIONS Read and answer each question.

1. Which types of words are always capitalized?

adjectives   brand names   food names

2. Add apostrophes to the sentence.

My dad shouldve told me that Jacks mom
was coming.

3. Add apostrophes to the following contractions.

whod   mustnt   isnt

4. Circle the adverb in the sentence.

Jessie arrived promptly as the school bell rang.

5. Write the past tense of the word in the blank.

Yesterday was the day I _____ my braces.
(get)

6. Circle the correctly spelled word.

age
aje
adg

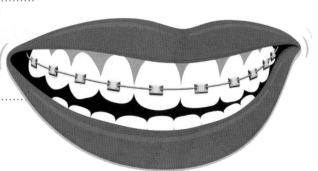

NAME: _____   **DATE:** _____

DIRECTIONS   Read and answer each question.

1. Circle the words that need capital letters.

The capital of our country is washington, d.c.

2. What is the proper way to greet someone in a letter?

Hello Mom;   Dear Mom,   Hi Mom!

3. Rewrite the sentence with a contraction.

December is not the best month for swimming in our pool.

_____

_____

4. Circle the adjectives in the sentence.

The frozen dessert was a treat on a hot day.

5. Write the plural noun to complete the sentence.

The dentist looked at my _____ to check for cavities.
(tooth)

6. Circle the word that is spelled correctly.

wheal   wheel   whel

1. Ⓨ Ⓝ

2. Ⓨ Ⓝ

3. Ⓨ Ⓝ

4. Ⓨ Ⓝ

5. Ⓨ Ⓝ

6. Ⓨ Ⓝ

___ / 6
Total

NAME: _____   **DATE:** _____

SCORE

1. Ⓨ Ⓝ

2. Ⓨ Ⓝ

3. Ⓨ Ⓝ

4. Ⓨ Ⓝ

5. Ⓨ Ⓝ

6. Ⓨ Ⓝ

___ / 6
Total

DIRECTIONS Read and answer each question.

1. Write a sentence about your favorite holiday memory using correct capitalization.

_____

_____

2. Circle the correct contraction.

we've   wv'e   weh've

3. Use an apostrophe to write *the mascot of the school* in another way.

_____

4. Many plural nouns end in *-s* or *-es*. Which noun does **not** follow this rule?

sheep   hat   adult

5. Circle the adverb in the sentence.

The kitten playfully swatted the ball of yarn.

6. Circle the correctly spelled word.

teecher

teacher

techer

NAME: _____ **DATE:** _____

DIRECTIONS Read and answer each question.

SCORE

1. Ⓨ Ⓝ

2. Ⓨ Ⓝ

3. Ⓨ Ⓝ

4. Ⓨ Ⓝ

5. Ⓨ Ⓝ

6. Ⓨ Ⓝ

___ / 6
Total

1. What brand of pizza do you like best? Write a sentence about it using correct capitalization.

_____

_____

2. Circle the contraction in the sentence.

Kids shouldn't spend too much time playing video games.

3. Add apostrophes to the following contractions.

Im   cant   couldve

4. What would you call a large number of students?

an army of students   a class of students   a troop of students

5. Write the correct pronoun to complete the sentence.

Our teacher told us to not grade _____ on the quiz.   (themselves, ourselves)

6. Circle the word that is spelled correctly.

strech   stritch   stretch

NAME: _____   **DATE:** _____

DIRECTIONS Read and answer each question.

1. Which word is always capitalized?

Arkansas   Dear   From

2. Use an apostrophe to write *the cookie from the bakery* in another way.

_____

3. Add commas to the letter.

Dear Owner
I was in your store today. Your employee was very helpful. We are so glad your store is near our house.
Sincerely
A happy customer

4. Write two adjectives about school.

_____   _____

5. Complete the sentence with a noun and a verb.

A herd of _____ went _____.

6. Circle the word that is spelled correctly.

shook   shouk   showk

NAME: _____ **DATE:** _____

DIRECTIONS Read and answer each question.

1. Circle the words that need capital letters.

Should we go to new orleans or fort lauderdale on our vacation?

2. Add an apostrophe to the sentence.

The postal worker cannot deliver to our house because of Shannons dog.

3. Rewrite the following words as contractions.

did not   could have   might not

_____   _____   _____

4. Circle the adverb in the sentence.

The girls moved quickly to catch the ice cream truck.

5. Write a noun in the blank that makes sense.

The pack of _____ roamed the land in search of food.

6. Circle the word that is spelled correctly.

layd   lade   laid

NAME: _____ DATE: _____

DIRECTIONS Read and answer each question.

1. What is the capital of your country?

1. Ⓨ Ⓝ

_____

2. Ⓨ Ⓝ

2. Add commas to this letter.

Dear Principal Smith
Would you consider having the cafeteria serve
dessert on Fridays? Please think about it.
Sincerely
Jaden

3. Ⓨ Ⓝ

4. Ⓨ Ⓝ

5. Ⓨ Ⓝ

3. Circle the correct contraction.

wer'e   wea've   wasn't

6. Ⓨ Ⓝ

4. Circle the adjectives in the sentence.

___/6
Total

The green grass grew quickly under
the warm sun.

5. Circle the plural noun in the sentence.

The fish were colorful in the ocean.

6. Write a word that has the same -igh
spelling pattern as in light.

_____

NAME: _____ DATE: _____

DIRECTIONS Read and answer each question.

1. Circle the word that needs a capital letter.

Some of my favorite movies are made by pixar®.

1. Ⓨ Ⓝ

2. Which contraction uses the apostrophe correctly?

ca'nt   they'll   Iv'e

2. Ⓨ Ⓝ

3. Ⓨ Ⓝ

3. Use an apostrophe to write *the lunch that belongs to Mario* in another way.

_____

4. Ⓨ Ⓝ

4. What would you call a large amount of fish?

a school   a pack   an army

5. Ⓨ Ⓝ

6. Ⓨ Ⓝ

5. Circle the adverb in the sentence.

The squirrel mischievously ate the nuts from the tree in our garden.

___ / 6
Total

6. Write a word that has the same *-ir* spelling pattern as in *skirt*.

_____

NAME: _____ DATE: _____

DIRECTIONS Read and answer each question.

1. Circle the word that needs a capital letter.

We really like to go to newport to stay at the beach.

2. Circle the contraction in the sentence.

We didn't see the lions at the zoo because they were napping.

3. Add an apostrophe to the sentence.

Veronicas homework was missing from her backpack.

4. What would you call a large amount of trees?

a forest   a colony   a deck

5. Write the correct pronoun to complete the sentence.

Mom said, "I want you to take care of your chores _____."
(myself, herself, yourself)

6. Circle the word that is spelled correctly.

sowk   soak   soke

NAME: _____ **DATE:** _____

DIRECTIONS Read and answer each question.

1. Which word is always capitalized?

Easter   First   Can't

1. Ⓨ Ⓝ

2. Use an apostrophe to write *the pizza from Yummy Pie* in another way.

_____

2. Ⓨ Ⓝ

3. Ⓨ Ⓝ

3. Add commas to the letter.

Dear Grandma
When are you coming for a visit? I miss you very much.
Love
Sofia

4. Ⓨ Ⓝ

5. Ⓨ Ⓝ

6. Ⓨ Ⓝ

4. Write an adjective to complete the sentence.

I didn't want my _____ birthday party to end.

___ / 6
Total

5. Complete the sentence with a noun and a verb.

A pack of _____ went _____.

6. Circle the word that is spelled correctly.

soap   sowp   soppe

NAME: _____ **DATE:** _____

SCORE

1. Ⓨ Ⓝ

2. Ⓨ Ⓝ

3. Ⓨ Ⓝ

4. Ⓨ Ⓝ

5. Ⓨ Ⓝ

6. Ⓨ Ⓝ

___ / 6
Total

DIRECTIONS Read and answer each question.

1. Which types of words are always capitalized?

days of the week   contractions   adverbs

2. Add apostrophes to the sentence.

Keegan cant believe that Jasons sister could be that mean.

3. Add apostrophes to the following contractions.

arent   shouldve   didnt

4. Circle the adverb in the sentence.

The airplane landed safely after a rough ride.

5. Write a noun in the blank.

The burglar stole a wad of _____ from my wallet.

6. Circle the word that is spelled correctly.

ubout   abowt   about

NAME: _____ **DATE:** _____

DIRECTIONS Read and answer each question.

1. Circle the words that need capital letters.

Pollution is harming the atlantic ocean.

1. Ⓨ Ⓝ

2. Rewrite the sentence with two contractions.

I do not know where I am going to eat lunch today.

2. Ⓨ Ⓝ

_____

3. Ⓨ Ⓝ

_____

4. Ⓨ Ⓝ

3. Use an apostrophe to write *the buttons on the coat* in another way.

5. Ⓨ Ⓝ

_____

6. Ⓨ Ⓝ

4. Circle the adjectives in the sentence.

I noticed the speeding car race down the street.

___ / 6
Total

5. Circle the plural noun in the sentence.

The mice scurried into the hole in the ground.

6. Write a word that has the same *-ow* spelling pattern as in *snow*.

_____

NAME: _____ **DATE:** _____

DIRECTIONS Read and answer each question.

1. Ⓨ Ⓝ

2. Ⓨ Ⓝ

3. Ⓨ Ⓝ

4. Ⓨ Ⓝ

5. Ⓨ Ⓝ

6. Ⓨ Ⓝ

___ / 6
Total

1. Circle the word that needs a capital letter.

I would like to visit paris, France.

2. Circle the correct contraction.

Im   I'm   Im'

3. Rewrite the sentence using an apostrophe.

The pool belonging to Mario felt very refreshing on a hot day.

_____

_____

4. Many plural nouns end in -s or -es. Which noun does **not** fit this rule?

cat   man   table

5. Circle the adverb in the sentence.

Scientists rarely see endangered species.

6. Write a word that has the same -oa spelling pattern as in *goat*.

_____

NAME: _____ **DATE:** _____

DIRECTIONS Read and answer each question.

1. What is the name of your favorite park? Write a sentence about it with correct capitalization.

_____

_____

2. Circle the contraction in the sentence.

Vanilla isn't my favorite choice for ice cream.

3. Add commas to the letter.

Dear Frank
Can you come over for a sleepover tonight?
Your friend
Marco

4. What would you call a large group of bees?

| a deck of bees | a swarm of bees | a bouquet of bees |

5. Circle the pronouns in the sentence.

What will you do with yourself over vacation?

6. Circle the word that is spelled correctly.

| poam | pome | poem |

1. Ⓨ Ⓝ

2. Ⓨ Ⓝ

3. Ⓨ Ⓝ

4. Ⓨ Ⓝ

5. Ⓨ Ⓝ

6. Ⓨ Ⓝ

___/6
Total

NAME: _____ DATE: _____

DIRECTIONS Read and answer each question.

1. Ⓨ Ⓝ

2. Ⓨ Ⓝ

3. Ⓨ Ⓝ

4. Ⓨ Ⓝ

5. Ⓨ Ⓝ

6. Ⓨ Ⓝ

___/ 6
Total

1. Which word is always capitalized?

Montana   From   Be

2. Use an apostrophe to write *the antenna on the ant* in another way.

_____

3. Circle the correct greeting for a letter.

Sincerely;   Love---   Dear Nancy,

4. Write an adverb that could be used in the sentence.

The butterfly flew _____ through the sky.

5. Complete the sentence with a noun and a verb.

A tribe of _____ went _____.

6. Circle the correctly spelled word.

grew
gru
greu

#51167—180 Days of Language

NAME: _____ DATE: _____

DIRECTIONS Read and answer each question.

1. What types of words are always capitalized?

months of the year   compound words   adjectives

2. Add apostrophes to the sentence.

Drivers dont always know that the cars gas is almost out.

3. Add apostrophes to the following contractions.

doesnt   wont   havent

4. Circle the adverb in the sentence.

My bus driver greets me cheerfully every morning.

5. Write the correct pronoun to complete the sentence.

I had to excuse _____ from the table.
(myself, herself, yourself)

6. Write a word that has the same -*alk* spelling pattern as in *talk*.

_____

NAME: _____ **DATE:** _____

SCORE

1. Ⓨ Ⓝ

2. Ⓨ Ⓝ

3. Ⓨ Ⓝ

4. Ⓨ Ⓝ

5. Ⓨ Ⓝ

6. Ⓨ Ⓝ

___ / 6
Total

DIRECTIONS Read and answer each question.

1. Circle the words that need capital letters.

Our vacation to london, england, was the best part of the summer.

2. How would you write a closing for a letter to a teacher?

_____

3. Circle the contraction in the sentence.

The students should've studied harder for the challenging test.

4. Circle the adjectives in the sentence.

The healthy plant continued to grow many leaves.

5. Circle the plural nouns.

The hostesses cut the cakes at parties.

6. Circle the word that has the same -*ai* sound as in *train*.

said
pair
grain

NAME: _____ **DATE:** _____

DIRECTIONS Read and answer each question.

1. Circle the words that need capital letters.

Where can I find park view school?

1. Ⓨ Ⓝ

2. Circle the correct contraction.

willn't   won't   will't

2. Ⓨ Ⓝ

3. Ⓨ Ⓝ

3. Use an apostrophe to write *the petal on the flower* in another way.

_____

4. Ⓨ Ⓝ

5. Ⓨ Ⓝ

4. Many plural nouns end in *-s* or *-es*. Which noun does **not** fit this rule?

book   computer   child

6. Ⓨ Ⓝ

5. Circle the adverb in the sentence.

The zookeeper talked excitedly about the new lions.

___ / 6
Total

6. Circle the word that has the same *-oe* sound as in *toe*.

does

shoe

goes

NAME: _____ DATE: _____

DIRECTIONS Read and answer each question.

1. Ⓨ Ⓝ

1. Circle the words that always need capital letters.

labor day   you   north pole   love

2. Ⓨ Ⓝ

2. Rewrite the sentence using an apostrophe.

The backyard that belongs to Chloe has the best swing set!

_____

_____

3. Ⓨ Ⓝ

4. Ⓨ Ⓝ

5. Ⓨ Ⓝ

3. Add commas to this letter.

Dear Mr. Evans
Our classroom really needs a new computer.
Sincerely
The students in room 5

6. Ⓨ Ⓝ

___/6
Total

4. What would you call a group of puppies?

a litter   a troop   a flock

5. Circle the pronoun in the sentence.

The elephant tried to cool itself with water.

6. Circle the word that is spelled correctly.

pleass   pleese   please

NAME: _____ **DATE:** _____

DIRECTIONS Read and answer each question.

1. Circle the words that need capital letters.

The view from the top of mount everest was the most beautiful thing I have ever seen.

1. Ⓨ Ⓝ

2. How can you rewrite *the dog that belongs to Shelly* using an apostrophe?

_____

2. Ⓨ Ⓝ

3. Ⓨ Ⓝ

3. Which letter greeting is correct?

Dear Felix?   Dear Felix,   Dear Felix!

4. Ⓨ Ⓝ

4. Write an adjective to complete the sentence.

Our _____ boat barely made it out of the dock.

5. Ⓨ Ⓝ

6. Ⓨ Ⓝ

5. Complete the sentence with a noun and an adverb.

A herd of _____ traveled _____.

___ / 6
Total

6. Circle the correctly spelled word.

rok
rawk
rock

NAME: _____ **DATE:** _____

DIRECTIONS Read and answer each question.

1. Circle the words that need capital letters.

The train will stop at the towns of jackson, hollywood, and parker.

2. Add apostrophes to the sentence.

Maria couldnt see that her sisters toy was under the bed.

3. Add apostrophes to the following contractions.

shouldnt   theyre   arent

4. Circle the adverb in the sentence.

Jose's mom divided the cookie evenly.

5. Complete the sentence with a noun and an adverb.

A swarm of _____ moved _____.

6. Write a word that has the same -ea spelling pattern as in sea.

_____

NAME: _____ **DATE:** _____

DIRECTIONS Read and answer each question.

1. Circle the words that need capital letters.

Henry wants to go to the amazon rainforest for new year's day.

2. What kind of greeting would you write in a letter to a friend?

_____

3. Rewrite the sentence with a contraction.

They are the best friends I could ever want.

_____

_____

4. Circle the adjectives in the sentence.

The warm muffin was on the menu at our special restaurant.

5. Write a sentence using the plural noun *children*.

_____

_____

6. Circle the word that is spelled correctly.

took   tuhk   toowk

1. Ⓨ Ⓝ

2. Ⓨ Ⓝ

3. Ⓨ Ⓝ

4. Ⓨ Ⓝ

5. Ⓨ Ⓝ

6. Ⓨ Ⓝ

___ / 6
Total

NAME: _____ **DATE:** _____

SCORE

DIRECTIONS Read and answer each question.

1. Why is *Crocs* capitalized in the sentence?

My Crocs® sandals are the best to wear to the beach.

_____

1. Ⓨ Ⓝ

2. Ⓨ Ⓝ

2. Which word means "who is"?

whose   who's   whos'

3. Ⓨ Ⓝ

4. Ⓨ Ⓝ

3. Use an apostrophe to write *the food that belongs to the cat* in another way.

_____

5. Ⓨ Ⓝ

6. Ⓨ Ⓝ

4. Many plural nouns end in -*s* or -*es*. Which noun does **not** fit this rule?

ring   mouse   hat

___ / 6
Total

5. Circle the adverbs in the sentence.

Kara lovingly hugged her brother before he quickly walked to the bus stop.

6. Circle the word that is spelled correctly.

wewl   wool   wowl

NAME: _____ **DATE:** _____

DIRECTIONS Read and answer each question.

1. Write a sentence about your favorite television show with correct capitalization.

_____

_____

2. Add a contraction to the sentence.

My sister got into trouble, and now _____ very sad.
(I am)

3. Write a closing for a letter to a close friend.

_____

4. What would you call a large number of animals?

a herd   a team   a range

5. Write the correct pronoun to complete the sentence.

Lily jumped in the puddle because she could not help _____.
(myself, herself, yourself)

6. Circle the word that has the same -oo spelling pattern as in *book*.

took   tool   boot

1. Ⓨ Ⓝ
2. Ⓨ Ⓝ
3. Ⓨ Ⓝ
4. Ⓨ Ⓝ
5. Ⓨ Ⓝ
6. Ⓨ Ⓝ

___ / 6
Total

NAME: _____ **DATE:** _____

DIRECTIONS Read and answer each question.

1. Which holiday is your least favorite, and why? Write a sentence about it with correct capitalization.

_____

_____

2. Use an apostrophe to write *the phone belonging to Pablo* in another way.

_____

3. Add commas to the letter.

Dear Mom
Thank you for the birthday party.
Love
Luke

4. Write an adjective to complete the sentence.

The _____ tea was served from a teapot.

5. Write a sentence using the word *bunch* to describe several objects.

_____

_____

6. Circle the word that is spelled correctly.

suth   sutch   such

NAME: _____ **DATE:** _____

DIRECTIONS Read and answer each question.

1. Circle the words that need capital letters.

Jack's favorite baseball team is from san francisco.

2. Add apostrophes to the sentence.

The teacher didnt want to give directions until the students talking had stopped.

3. Add apostrophes to the following contractions.

Ill   couldnt   shell

4. Circle the adverb in the sentence.

Good friends almost always play happily together.

5. Complete the sentence with a noun and a verb..

A litter of _____ went _____.

6. Circle the correctly spelled word.

howr
hour
houer

NAME: _____ **DATE:** _____

DIRECTIONS Read and answer each question.

1. Circle the words that need capital letters.

Check the weather in springfield and salem.

2. Write a greeting for a letter to your neighbor.

_____

3. Rewrite the sentence with two contractions.

I would like to sing, but I cannot sing in class.

_____

_____

4. Circle the adjectives in the sentence.

The happy baby wanted to crawl to the exciting toy.

5. Rewrite the sentence in the past tense.

I keep a diary of what I do each day.

_____

_____

6. Write another word that has the same -ink spelling pattern as in sink.

_____

NAME: _____ **DATE:** _____

DIRECTIONS Read and answer each question.

1. Circle the words that need capital letters.

The video game can work on microsoft® or apple® machines.

1. Ⓨ Ⓝ

2. Ⓨ Ⓝ

2. Circle the correct contraction

howl'd howl'ld how'd

3. Ⓨ Ⓝ

3. Use an apostrophe to write *the leg of the chair* in another way.

_____

4. Ⓨ Ⓝ

5. Ⓨ Ⓝ

4. Rewrite the sentence in the past tense.

I see the customer pay for the groceries.

_____

_____

6. Ⓨ Ⓝ

___ / 6
Total

5. Circle the adverbs in the sentence.

The rain fell quietly while I slept peacefully in my bed.

6. Write another word that has the same -*ing* spelling pattern as in *ring*.

_____

NAME: _____ **DATE:** _____

DIRECTIONS Read and answer each question.

SCORE

1. Y N

2. Y N

3. Y N

4. Y N

5. Y N

6. Y N

___ / 6
Total

1. Write a sentence about a holiday you celebrate using correct capitalization.

_____

_____

2. Write the contraction in the sentence.

Rap music _____ be played at school.
(should not)

3. Write a closing in a letter to a family member.

_____

4. What would you call several drawers?

a chest of drawers   a troop of drawers   a string of drawers

5. Write the correct pronoun to complete the sentence.

The door was unlocked, so we let _____ in the house.
(ourselves, yourselves)

6. Write another word that has the same -*ar* spelling pattern as in *farm*.

_____

NAME: _____   **DATE:** _____

DIRECTIONS Read and answer each question.

1. Write the name of a place that always starts with a capital letter.

_____

1. Ⓨ Ⓝ

2. Use an apostrophe to write *keys on a piano* in another way.

_____

2. Ⓨ Ⓝ

3. Ⓨ Ⓝ

3. Add commas to the letter.

Dear neighbor
I accidentally hit the ball through your window.
I can help you fix it.
Your neighbor
Henry

4. Ⓨ Ⓝ

5. Ⓨ Ⓝ

6. Ⓨ Ⓝ

4. Write an adjective to complete the sentence.

Our _____ dog always greets us when we come home.

___/6
Total

5. Complete the sentence with a noun and an adverb.

A choir of _____ sounded _____.

6. Circle the word that is spelled correctly.

taile   tail   tayl

NAME: _____ DATE: _____

SCORE

1. Ⓨⓝ

2. Ⓨⓝ

3. Ⓨⓝ

4. Ⓨⓝ

5. Ⓨⓝ

6. Ⓨⓝ

___/6
Total

DIRECTIONS Read and answer each question.

1. Write the name of a holiday that always starts with a capital letter.

_____

2. Write a greeting for the letter.

_____

I would like to request that Johnson Park stay open. Closing this park would make many people very sad, including me.

3. Write a closing for the letter above.

_____

_____

4. Write a sentence about how you got to school today using an adverb.

_____

_____

5. Write a sentence about what you are wearing today using an adjective.

_____

_____

6. Circle the word that is spelled correctly.

meet   meit   meyt

NAME: _____ DATE: _____

DIRECTIONS Read and answer each question.

1. Circle the words that need capital letters.

The airplane flew from las vegas to new york.

2. Add commas to this letter.

Dear Coach
I learned a lot about soccer from you.
Your player
Romeo

3. Circle the correct contraction.

theyd'e   the'yre   they'll

4. Circle the adjectives in the sentence.

Naomi slept with her fluffy bear on a stormy night.

5. Write the plural noun to complete the sentence.

Basketball _____ are 12 minutes each.
(half)

6. Write a word that has the same spelling pattern as -*ay* in *day*.

_____

NAME: _____ DATE: _____

DIRECTIONS Read and answer each question.

1. Circle the words that need capital letters.

My mom buys the healthy cereal made by nature's best®.

2. Which contraction uses the apostrophe correctly?

shes'   wer'e   who'll

3. Use an apostrophe to write *the coat that belongs to Mariela* in another way.

_____

4. What would you call several mountains?

a mountain   a mountain   a mountain
range   team   pack

5. Circle the adverb in the sentence.

The bicycle went by quickly as it went down the hill.

6. Write a word that has the same spelling pattern as *-ai* in *pain*.

_____

NAME: _____ **DATE:** _____

DIRECTIONS Read and answer each question.

1. Circle the words that need capital letters.

The red sea is amazing to see.

1. Ⓨ Ⓝ

2. Circle the contraction in the sentence.

He's my best friend, so I chose him to be on my team.

2. Ⓨ Ⓝ

3. Ⓨ Ⓝ

3. Add an apostrophe to the sentence.

Jacks baseball team made the playoffs.

4. Ⓨ Ⓝ

5. Ⓨ Ⓝ

4. What would you call a group of soccer players?

pack   staff   team

6. Ⓨ Ⓝ

___ / 6
Total

5. Write the correct pronoun to complete the sentence.

Violet said, "Can you please take care of our
puppy _____?"
(myself, herself, yourself)

6. Write a word that has the same spelling pattern as -aw in saw.

_____

NAME: _____ **DATE:** _____

DIRECTIONS Read and answer each question.

1. Which word is always capitalized?

Thanksgiving   Too   Turtle

2. Use an apostrophe to write *the prey of the lion* in another way.

_____

3. Add commas to the letter.

Dear Dad
I am very sorry that I lost your keys.
I will help you find them.
Your son
Pablo

4. Write two adjectives to complete the sentence.

The _____, _____
sunrise was beautiful to watch.

5. Complete the sentence with a noun and a verb.

A flock of _____ went _____.

6. Write a word that has the same *-oo* spelling pattern as in *root*.

_____

NAME: _____ **DATE:** _____

DIRECTIONS   Read and answer each question.

1. What types of words are always capitalized?

colors   verbs   proper nouns

2. Add apostrophes to the sentence.

Lukes birthday guest list includes Leo and Leos sister.

3. Add apostrophes to the following contractions.

wheres   howd   youve

4. Write an adverb to complete the sentence.

The cat moved _____ across the lawn.

5. Circle the plural noun in the sentence.

A group of men worked together to push the car.

6. Circle the correctly spelled word.

boowt
boote
boot

NAME: _____ DATE: _____

DIRECTIONS Read and answer each question.

1. (Y)(N)

2. (Y)(N)

3. (Y)(N)

4. (Y)(N)

5. (Y)(N)

6. (Y)(N)

___ / 6
Total

1. Write the name of a city.

_____

2. What is another way to write *the pet of a friend*?

a friend's pet   a friends pet   a friend,s pet

3. Which contraction is spelled correctly?

I'ts   Il'l   I'm

4. Write an adjective to complete the sentence.

The _____ bird was easy to spot in the tree.

5. Write the plural noun to complete the sentence.

_____ are great places to visit.
(City)

6. Write a word that has the same -*oy* spelling pattern as in *boy*.

_____

NAME: _____ DATE: _____

Read and answer each question.

SCORE

1. Circle the words that need capital letters.

The book was just published by teacher created materials®.

2. What is another way to write *the hair of a mom*?

mom's hair   moms hair   moms' hair

3. Use an apostrophe to write *the ice cream belonging to Ted* in another way.

_____

4. Write an adverb to complete the sentence.

The turbo jet flew _____ across the sky.

5. Circle the adverb in the sentence.

The door creaked slowly as I opened it.

6. Write a word that has the same *-oi* spelling pattern as in *soil*.

_____

1. Ⓨ Ⓝ

2. Ⓨ Ⓝ

3. Ⓨ Ⓝ

4. Ⓨ Ⓝ

5. Ⓨ Ⓝ

6. Ⓨ Ⓝ

___ / 6
Total

NAME: _____ **DATE:** _____

SCORE

1. Ⓨ Ⓝ

2. Ⓨ Ⓝ

3. Ⓨ Ⓝ

4. Ⓨ Ⓝ

5. Ⓨ Ⓝ

6. Ⓨ Ⓝ

___ / 6
Total

DIRECTIONS Read and answer each question.

1. Circle the words that need capital letters.

The police went to north hanford on a call.

2. Write the contraction to complete the sentence.

_____ Ana not in school today?
(Why is)

3. Add an apostrophe to the sentence.

Aidens turn on the computer is today.

4. What would you call a large amount of sailors?

a choir   a crew   a class

5. Write the correct pronoun to complete the sentence.

"I will just do it _____," Sara said.
(myself, herself, yourself)

6. Write a word that has the same -*age* spelling pattern as in *cage*.

_____

NAME: _____ **DATE:** _____

DIRECTIONS Read and answer each question.

1. Which word is always capitalized?

Colorado   You   Restaurant

1. Ⓨ Ⓝ

2. Use an apostrophe to write *the toy car belonging to Oscar* in another way.

_____

2. Ⓨ Ⓝ

3. Ⓨ Ⓝ

3. Add commas to the letter.

Dear George
Will you bring your trucks to our play date?
Your friend
Jeffrey

4. Ⓨ Ⓝ

5. Ⓨ Ⓝ

6. Ⓨ Ⓝ

4. Write the correct verb to complete the sentence.

The student _____ at a new desk yesterday.
(sitting, sat, sitted)

___/6
Total

5. Complete the sentence with two nouns.

A team of _____ wanted _____.

6. Circle the word that is spelled correctly.

cave   kave   ckave

NAME: _____ **DATE:** _____

SCORE

DIRECTIONS Read and answer each question.

1. Ⓨ Ⓝ

1. What types of words are always capitalized?

cities   color words   plurals

2. Ⓨ Ⓝ

2. Add apostrophes to the sentence.

Dad couldnt go to Sarahs game today.

3. Ⓨ Ⓝ

3. Add apostrophes to the following contractions.

mustnt   hadnt   arent

4. Ⓨ Ⓝ

4. Write the correct verb to complete the sentence.

Jesse _____ under the bed to trick his mom.
(hid, hiding, hided)

5. Ⓨ Ⓝ

5. Write the plural noun to complete the sentence.

The _____ loved the summer camp.
(child)

6. Ⓨ Ⓝ

___ / 6
Total

6. Circle the correctly spelled word.

kick

cick

ckick

 #51167—180 Days of Language

NAME: _____ **DATE:** _____

DIRECTIONS Read and answer each question.

1. Circle the words that need capital letters.

Have you ever been to west virginia?

1. Ⓨ Ⓝ

2. Write a greeting for the letter.

_____

Our school garden is finally growing food! We have worked very hard on it. Thank you for your help.

2. Ⓨ Ⓝ

3. Ⓨ Ⓝ

3. Write a closing for the letter above.

_____

_____

4. Ⓨ Ⓝ

4. Circle the adjectives in the sentence.

The yellow flower poked out of the wet soil.

5. Ⓨ Ⓝ

6. Ⓨ Ⓝ

___ / 6
Total

5. Write the plural noun to complete the sentence.

The _____ read books to relax.
(woman)

6. Write a word that has the same -y spelling pattern as in *cry*.

_____

NAME: _____   DATE: _____

SCORE

DIRECTIONS   Read and answer each question.

1. Ⓨ Ⓝ

1. Circle the words that need capital letters.

My favorite gift was blocks made by lego®.

2. Ⓨ Ⓝ

2. Which contraction uses the apostrophe correctly?

shouldv'e   could've   mightv'e

3. Ⓨ Ⓝ

3. Use an apostrophe to write *the candy that belongs to Fred* in another way.

4. Ⓨ Ⓝ

_____

5. Ⓨ Ⓝ

4. What would you call a large group of horses that work together.

6. Ⓨ Ⓝ

a team   a swarm   a mob

____/ 6
Total

5. Circle the adverb in the sentence.

We have to leave soon to get a table.

6. Write a word that has the same -*ate* spelling pattern as in *late*.

_____

NAME: _____ **DATE:** _____

DIRECTIONS Read and answer each question.

1. Circle the word that needs a capital letter.

There are many deserts in arizona.

1. Ⓨ Ⓝ

2. Write the contraction to complete the sentence.

_____ meet us at the concert.
(They will)

2. Ⓨ Ⓝ

3. Ⓨ Ⓝ

3. Add an apostrophe to the sentence.

Jacksons skateboard was brand new.

4. Ⓨ Ⓝ

5. Ⓨ Ⓝ

4. Fill in the blanks with words that make sense.

a class of   a team of

_____   _____

6. Ⓨ Ⓝ

___ / 6
Total

5. Write the correct pronoun to complete the sentence.

Grace said, "You cannot vote for _____
in this game."   (itself, myself, yourself)

6. Circle the word that is spelled correctly.

lodge   loj   lohj

NAME: _____ **DATE:** _____

SCORE

1. Ⓨ Ⓝ

2. Ⓨ Ⓝ

3. Ⓨ Ⓝ

4. Ⓨ Ⓝ

5. Ⓨ Ⓝ

6. Ⓨ Ⓝ

___ / 6
Total

DIRECTIONS Read and answer each question.

1. Circle the words that are always capitalized.

America   You   Street   Africa

2. Use an apostrophe to write *the water that belongs to Chloe* in another way.

_____

3. Add commas to the letter.

Dear Mom
Happy Mother's Day! You are the best.
Love
Nina

4. Write two adjectives to complete the sentence.

This _____, _____
vacation is a lot of fun.

5. Write a sentence using the word *herd* to describe an animal group.

_____

_____

6. Circle the word that is spelled correctly.

soile   soyl   soil

NAME: _____   DATE: _____

DIRECTIONS   Read and answer each question.

1. Which types of words are always capitalized?

pronouns   compound   countries
                  words

2. Add apostrophes to the sentence.

Harpers dog shouldnt be off the leash.

3. Add apostrophes to the following contractions.

Ive   were   mustnt

4. Circle the adverb in the sentence.

She is nearly six years old because her birthday is next week.

5. Write the plural noun to complete the sentence.

The _____ played football all morning.
        (man)

6. Circle the word that is spelled correctly.

slepe   sleap   sleep

1. Ⓨ Ⓝ

2. Ⓨ Ⓝ

3. Ⓨ Ⓝ

4. Ⓨ Ⓝ

5. Ⓨ Ⓝ

6. Ⓨ Ⓝ

___ / 6
Total

NAME: _____ DATE: _____

DIRECTIONS Read and answer each question.

SCORE

1. Ⓨ Ⓝ

2. Ⓨ Ⓝ

3. Ⓨ Ⓝ

4. Ⓨ Ⓝ

5. Ⓨ Ⓝ

6. Ⓨ Ⓝ

___ / 6
Total

1. Circle the words that need capital letters.

Is anyone able to visit the south pole?

2. What is another way to write *the owner of a restaurant*?

| the restaurants' owner | the restaurant's owner | the restaurants owner |

3. Which contraction is spelled correctly?

mustn't   could'nt   were'nt

4. Circle the adjectives in the sentence.

The blue bird sat on a small branch.

5. Write the plural noun to complete the sentence.

My dentist wants me to take care of my

_____ .
              (tooth)

6. Circle the word that is spelled correctly.

when   wen   whan

NAME: _____ **DATE:** _____

DIRECTIONS Read and answer each question.

SCORE

1. Ⓨ Ⓝ

2. Ⓨ Ⓝ

3. Ⓨ Ⓝ

4. Ⓨ Ⓝ

5. Ⓨ Ⓝ

6. Ⓨ Ⓝ

___ / 6
Total

1. Circle the word that needs a capital letter.

I really love toys made by the lego® company.

2. Which contraction uses the apostrophe correctly?

could'nt   theyr'e   I'll

3. Use an apostrophe to write *the food that belongs to the lion* in another way.

_____

4. What would you call a large amount of dogs?

a tribe   a herd   a pack

5. Circle the adverb in the sentence.

Stephanie shyly asked to borrow the jacket.

6. Circle the correctly spelled word.

sudge
sutch
such

NAME: _____ DATE: _____

SCORE

1. Y N

2. Y N

3. Y N

4. Y N

5. Y N

6. Y N

___ / 6
Total

DIRECTIONS Read and answer each question.

1. Circle the word that needs a capital letter.

The beaches in florida are quite pretty.

2. Write the contraction to complete the sentence.

We _____ leave you alone!
(would not)

3. Add an apostrophe to the sentence.

Jacobs football had no air.

4. What would you call a large group of wolves?

a pack   a flock   a litter

5. Write the correct pronoun to complete the sentence.

Dad shouted, "Take good care of _____,
Iris!"   (myself, herself, yourself)

6. Circle the correctly spelled word.

loyal
loil
loyl

NAME: _____ **DATE:** _____

DIRECTIONS Read and answer each question.

SCORE

1. Which word is always capitalized?

State　　　　　City　　　　　Chicago

1. Ⓨ Ⓝ

2. Use an apostrophe to write *the ticket that belongs to Brady* in another way.

_____

2. Ⓨ Ⓝ

3. Ⓨ Ⓝ

3. Add commas to the letter.

Dear Luis
Will you come to my party? It is on Saturday.
Your friend
Sam

4. Ⓨ Ⓝ

4. Write an adjective that makes sense in the sentence.

The _____ waves crashed loudly.

5. Ⓨ Ⓝ

6. Ⓨ Ⓝ

___ / 6
Total

5. Write the correct verb to complete the sentence.

Parker _____ a secret to his sister.
　　　　(telling, telled, told)

6. Circle the word that is spelled correctly.

muge　　　　　much　　　　　mutch

NAME: _____ **DATE:** _____

SCORE

1. Ⓨ Ⓝ

2. Ⓨ Ⓝ

3. Ⓨ Ⓝ

4. Ⓨ Ⓝ

5. Ⓨ Ⓝ

6. Ⓨ Ⓝ

___/ 6
Total

DIRECTIONS Read and answer each question.

1. What types of words are always capitalized?

city names   compound   adjectives
                    words

2. Add apostrophes to the sentence.

Dont you want to go to Milos party?

3. Add apostrophes to the following contractions.

Ive   mustnt   theyll

4. Circle the adverb in the sentence.

I partially opened the window to let in cool air.

5. Write the correct verb to complete the sentence.

Our class _____ for our school picture.
            (sitting, sat, sitted)

6. Circle the word that is spelled correctly.

late   laet   layt

NAME: _____ **DATE:** _____

DIRECTIONS Read and answer each question.

1. Circle the words that need capital letters.

The boat sailed on the indian ocean.

1. Ⓨ Ⓝ

2. Rewrite the sentence with two contractions.

The cat does not see that she is sitting on a toy.

_____

_____

2. Ⓨ Ⓝ

3. Ⓨ Ⓝ

4. Ⓨ Ⓝ

3. Use an apostrophe to write *the roof on the house* in another way.

_____

5. Ⓨ Ⓝ

6. Ⓨ Ⓝ

4. Circle the adjectives in the sentence.

The happy man smiled at his young child.

___ / 6
Total

5. Write the plural noun to complete the sentence.

Sam's _____ were hurting.
(foot)

6. Write a word that has the same -*sk* spelling pattern as in *mask*.

_____

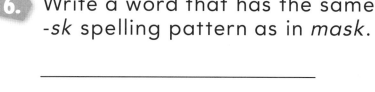

NAME: _____ **DATE:** _____

SCORE

1. Ⓨ Ⓝ

2. Ⓨ Ⓝ

3. Ⓨ Ⓝ

4. Ⓨ Ⓝ

5. Ⓨ Ⓝ

6. Ⓨ Ⓝ

___ / 6
Total

DIRECTIONS Read and answer each question.

1. Circle the words that need capital letters.

My favorite show is on cartoon network®.

2. Which word means "they are"?

their   they're   there

3. Rewrite the sentence using an apostrophe.

The leash on the dog was too tight.

_____

_____

4. Many plural nouns end in *-s* or *-es*. Which noun does **not** fit this rule?

flower   glass   goose

5. Circle the adverb in the sentence.

Mom calmly told me to come inside.

6. Write a word that has the same *-ea* spelling pattern as in *mean*.

_____

#51167—*180 Days of Language*   © Shell Education

NAME: _____ **DATE:** _____

DIRECTIONS Read and answer each question.

1. Circle the words that need capital letters.

There are many old buildings in rome, italy.

2. Add a contraction to complete the sentence.

The store _____ be open today.
(must not)

3. Write a greeting and a closing for the letter.

_____

Thank you for the present. I love it. I had a great
birthday.

_____

_____

4. What is a large group of cows called?

a team   a herd   a class

5. Circle the pronouns in the sentence.

Jade hurt herself when she fell.

6. Circle the word that is spelled correctly.

height   hite   hight

NAME: _____ DATE: _____

DIRECTIONS Read and answer each question.

SCORE

1. Ⓨ Ⓝ

2. Ⓨ Ⓝ

3. Ⓨ Ⓝ

4. Ⓨ Ⓝ

5. Ⓨ Ⓝ

6. Ⓨ Ⓝ

___ / 6
Total

1. Which word is always capitalized?

Iowa   City   Brand

2. Use an apostrophe to write *the edge of the rock* in another way.

_____

3. Circle the correct greeting for a letter.

Sincerely,   Hi!   Dear Sasha,

4. Circle the adjectives in the sentence.

The lifelong friends watched the intense game.

5. Circle the adverb in the sentence.

We cheered loudly to support our team.

6. Circle the correctly spelled word.

three
threa
thre

NAME: _____ DATE: _____

DIRECTIONS Read and answer each question.

1. Which types of words are always capitalized?

sight words   names of cities   adjectives

2. Add apostrophes to the sentence.

Harry isnt afraid of Peters dog.

3. Add apostrophes to the contractions.

couldnt   theyll   wheres

4. Circle the adverb in the sentence.

The lock fit tightly on the door.

5. Write the correct pronoun to complete the sentence.

I should clean _____ up before I go
to sleep.   (myself, herself, yourself)

6. Write a word that has the same
-*age* spelling pattern as in *page*.

_____

1. Ⓨ Ⓝ

2. Ⓨ Ⓝ

3. Ⓨ Ⓝ

4. Ⓨ Ⓝ

5. Ⓨ Ⓝ

6. Ⓨ Ⓝ

___/6
Total

NAME: _____ **DATE:** _____

SCORE

DIRECTIONS Read and answer each question.

1. Circle the words that need capital letters.

Where is the nile river?

1. Ⓨ Ⓝ

2. Rewrite the sentence with a contraction.

I must not get a bad report from my teacher.

2. Ⓨ Ⓝ

_____

_____

3. Ⓨ Ⓝ

4. Ⓨ Ⓝ

3. Use an apostrophe to write *the lid of the pot* in another way.

5. Ⓨ Ⓝ

_____

6. Ⓨ Ⓝ

4. Circle the adjectives in the sentence.

The shiny penny stuck out of the sandy beach.

___ / 6
Total

5. Write the plural noun to complete the sentence.

The _____ boarded the bus at the stop.
(woman)

6. Write a word that has the same -*sh* spelling pattern as in *dash*.

_____

NAME: _____ **DATE:** _____

DIRECTIONS Read and answer each question.

1. Circle the word that needs a capital letter.

I love to watch cartoons on nickelodeon™.

1. Ⓨ Ⓝ

2. Which contraction means "she has"?

she'd   she'll   she's

2. Ⓨ Ⓝ

3. Rewrite the sentence using an apostrophe.

The dog belonging to Nola ran on the beach.

_____

_____

3. Ⓨ Ⓝ

4. Ⓨ Ⓝ

5. Ⓨ Ⓝ

6. Ⓨ Ⓝ

4. Many plural nouns end in *-s* or *-es*. Which noun does **not** fit this rule?

lip   hair   mouse

___ / 6
Total

5. Circle the adverb in the sentence.

The dolphin dove deeply in the water.

6. Write a word that has the same *-ft* spelling pattern as in *soft*.

_____

NAME: _____ **DATE:** _____

| DIRECTIONS | Read and answer each question. |

1. (Y)(N)

1. Write the name of a city or state. Remember to use a capital letter.

_____

2. (Y)(N)

2. Circle the contraction in the sentence.

Who'd like to have dessert tonight?

3. (Y)(N)

3. Write a greeting and a closing for the letter.

4. (Y)(N)

_____

My class is having a bake sale. There will be lots of goodies. Would you like to come?

5. (Y)(N)

_____

6. (Y)(N)

_____

___/6
Total

4. Complete the sentence with a noun and an adverb.

A stack of _____ fell _____.

5. Complete the sentence with a verb.

I can _____ all by myself.

6. Write a word that has the same -*ly* spelling pattern as in *badly*.

_____

NAME: _____ **DATE:** _____

DIRECTIONS Read and answer each question.

1. Circle the words that need capital letters.

The boat ride on lake erie was very peaceful.

1. Ⓨ Ⓝ

2. Use an apostrophe to write *the apple belonging to Hank* in another way.

2. Ⓨ Ⓝ

_____

3. Ⓨ Ⓝ

3. Circle the correct greeting for a letter.

Dear Sid,   Hey there!   Your friend:

4. Ⓨ Ⓝ

4. Write an adjective to complete the sentence.

The_____ gift at my party was my favorite.

5. Ⓨ Ⓝ

6. Ⓨ Ⓝ

5. Complete the sentence with a noun and a verb.

A group of _____ were _____.

___ / 6
Total

6. Write a word that has the same *-gh* spelling pattern as in *laugh*.

_____

NAME: _____ DATE: _____

DIRECTIONS Read and answer each question.

1. Write an example for each category.

a city: _____   a state: _____

2. Add apostrophes to the sentence.

A giraffes neck cant fit in a short building.

3. Add apostrophes to the following contractions.

Im   youve   youll

4. Write the correct verb to complete the sentence.

Who _____ at the table this morning?
(sitting, sat, sitted)

5. Circle the plural noun in the sentence.

The women ate lunch and then went back to work.

6. Circle the correctly spelled word.

tuff
tough
tugh

NAME: _____ **DATE:** _____

DIRECTIONS Read and answer each question.

1. Circle the words that need capital letters.

The sun sets over the pacific ocean.

2. Rewrite the sentence with two contractions.

I do not know where I will go after school.

_____

_____

3. Use an apostrophe to write *the bike belonging to Jack* in another way.

_____

4. Circle the adjectives in the sentence.

Diego wants warm soup for his birthday dinner.

5. Rewrite the sentence using a plural noun.

The tooth is very loose.

_____

_____

6. Write a word that has the same -*est* ending as in *fastest.*

_____

NAME: _____ **DATE:** _____

SCORE

1. Ⓨ Ⓝ

2. Ⓨ Ⓝ

3. Ⓨ Ⓝ

4. Ⓨ Ⓝ

5. Ⓨ Ⓝ

6. Ⓨ Ⓝ

___ / 6
Total

DIRECTIONS Read and answer each question.

1. Circle the word that needs a capital letter.

Our computer lab has microsoft® software.

2. Circle the correct contraction.

couldn't   could'nt   couldnt'

3. Rewrite the sentence using an apostrophe.

The doll belonging to Rita is very cute.

_____

_____

4. What are the plural forms of these nouns?

man   woman

_____   _____

5. Circle the adverb in the sentence.

Nora weighs exactly 70 pounds.

6. Write a word that has the same
-*ful* spelling pattern as in *hopeful*.

_____

NAME: _____ DATE: _____

DIRECTIONS Read and answer each question.

1. Circle the word that needs a capital letter.

The police officer from hartford was on patrol.

2. Circle the contraction in the sentence.

Some insects aren't cute and cuddly.

3. Write a greeting and a closing for the letter.

_____

Can you come to my class play? I would love to see you there. My mom and dad are going, too.

_____

_____

4. Write an adjective to complete the sentence.

I chose the _____ shirt to wear to school.

5. Circle the pronoun in the sentence.

"Take care of yourself and feel better," Maria told Ana.

6. Circle the word that is spelled correctly.

moost   most   moust

1. Ⓨ Ⓝ

2. Ⓨ Ⓝ

3. Ⓨ Ⓝ

4. Ⓨ Ⓝ

5. Ⓨ Ⓝ

6. Ⓨ Ⓝ

___ / 6
Total

NAME: _____   DATE: _____

DIRECTIONS Read and answer each question.

SCORE

1. Ⓨ Ⓝ

2. Ⓨ Ⓝ

3. Ⓨ Ⓝ

4. Ⓨ Ⓝ

5. Ⓨ Ⓝ

6. Ⓨ Ⓝ

__ / 6
Total

1. Circle the word that needs a capital letter.

Can I have quaker® oatmeal for breakfast?

2. Use an apostrophe to write *the spots on the leopard* in another way.

_____

3. Circle the correct greeting for a letter.

Sincerely;   Love---   Dear Ava,

4. Write an adverb to complete the sentence.

The baby crawled _____ on the floor.

5. Complete the sentence with a noun and a verb.

A crowd of _____ were _____.

6. Circle the correctly spelled word.

ocean

oshean

oshun

NAME: _____   **DATE:** _____

DIRECTIONS Read and answer each question.

1. Circle the word that needs a capital letter.

Where is wisconsin on the map?

1. Ⓨ Ⓝ

2. Add apostrophes to the sentence.

Shes always safe on her sisters bike.

2. Ⓨ Ⓝ

3. Ⓨ Ⓝ

3. Add apostrophes to the following contractions.

couldnt   mustve   isnt

4. Ⓨ Ⓝ

4. Circle the adverb in the sentence.

My mom greets me happily each day.

5. Ⓨ Ⓝ

6. Ⓨ Ⓝ

5. Write the plural noun to complete the sentence.

The _____ in class all sat still.
    (child)

___/6
Total

6. Write a word that has the same
-able spelling pattern as in *valuable*.

_____

NAME: _____ **DATE:** _____

SCORE

1. Y N

2. Y N

3. Y N

4. Y N

5. Y N

6. Y N

___ / 6
Total

DIRECTIONS Read and answer each question.

1. Circle the words that need capital letters.

The mississippi river flows for many miles.

2. Rewrite the sentence with two contractions.

I cannot eat the cookie because I am full.

_____

_____

3. Use an apostrophe to write *the sweater on Olivia* in another way.

_____

4. Circle the adjectives in the sentence.

The surprise party was a fun event.

5. Write the plural noun to complete the sentence.

The _____ lived on the farm.
         (goose)

6. Write a word that has the same *-ight* spelling pattern as in *might*.

_____

NAME: _____ **DATE:** _____

> **DIRECTIONS** Read and answer each question.

1. Circle the word that needs a capital letter.

I want to order a book from the scholastic® book order.

1. Ⓨ Ⓝ

2. Circle the correct contraction.

wh'os   who'se   who's

2. Ⓨ Ⓝ

3. Ⓨ Ⓝ

3. Rewrite the sentence using an apostrophe.

The bike belonging to Sophia is not working.

_____

_____

4. Ⓨ Ⓝ

5. Ⓨ Ⓝ

6. Ⓨ Ⓝ

4. Many plural nouns end in *-s* or *-es*. Which noun does **not** fit this rule?

deer   friend   team

___/6
Total

5. Circle the adverb in the sentence.

I walk my dog daily.

6. Circle the word that is spelled correctly.

trew   troo   true

NAME: _____ DATE: _____

DIRECTIONS Read and answer each question.

1. Write a sentence about a continent using correct capitalization.

_____

_____

2. Write a greeting for the letter.

_____

Thank you for my birthday present. I love the books. How did you know I liked to read these mysteries?

3. Write a closing for the letter above.

_____

_____

4. Circle the adjectives in the sentence.

The young child danced to the loud music.

5. Circle the adverb in the sentence.

The boy excitedly greeted his neighbor.

6. Circle the word that is spelled correctly.

tight   tiete   tite

  #51167—180 Days of Language

NAME: _____ **DATE:** _____

> **DIRECTIONS** Read and answer each question.

1. Write a sentence about where you were born using correct capitalization.

_____

1. Ⓨ Ⓝ

2. Write the contraction to complete the sentence.

_____ you get home from school?
(How will)

2. Ⓨ Ⓝ

3. Ⓨ Ⓝ

3. Circle the correct closing for a letter.

Sincerely,   Love---   Your friend;

4. Ⓨ Ⓝ

4. Write an adverb to complete the sentence.

The ship sailed _____ on the water.

5. Ⓨ Ⓝ

6. Ⓨ Ⓝ

5. Complete the sentence with a noun and an adverb.

A school of _____ moved _____.

___ / 6
Total

6. Circle the correctly spelled word.

heero

hearo

hero

NAME: _____ **DATE:** _____

SCORE

1. Ⓨ Ⓝ

2. Ⓨ Ⓝ

3. Ⓨ Ⓝ

4. Ⓨ Ⓝ

5. Ⓨ Ⓝ

6. Ⓨ Ⓝ

___ / 6
Total

DIRECTIONS Read and answer each question.

1. Which types of words are always capitalized?

names of countries   compound words   adjectives

2. Add apostrophes to the sentence.

The ships captain cant stop working while sailing.

3. Write the following contractions.

cannot   I have   she is

_____   _____   _____

4. Circle the adjectives in the sentence.

The long worm slithered through the warm ground.

5. Circle the adverb in the sentence.

The caterpillar moves slowly on the leaf.

6. Write a word that has the same -*ue* spelling pattern as in *blue*.

_____

NAME: _____ **DATE:** _____

DIRECTIONS Read and answer each question.

1. Circle the words that need capital letters.

Can you canoe on lake michigan?

1. Ⓨ Ⓝ

2. Rewrite the sentence with a contraction and apostrophes.

You will not come with me to Jans party?

_____

_____

2. Ⓨ Ⓝ

3. Ⓨ Ⓝ

4. Ⓨ Ⓝ

3. Use an apostrophe to write *the piano belonging to Erik* in another way.

_____

5. Ⓨ Ⓝ

6. Ⓨ Ⓝ

4. Circle the adjectives in the sentence.

I ate the delicious blueberry muffin.

___/6
Total

5. Circle the adverb in the sentence.

I quickly ate my breakfast.

6. Write a word that has the same -*mp* spelling pattern as in *camp*.

_____

NAME: _____ **DATE:** _____

SCORE

DIRECTIONS Read and answer each question.

1. Circle the word that needs a capital letter.

1. Ⓨ Ⓝ

Does this store sell levi® jeans?

2. Ⓨ Ⓝ

2. Which contraction means "you will"?

3. Ⓨ Ⓝ

you've   you'd   you'll

3. Rewrite the sentence using an apostrophe.

4. Ⓨ Ⓝ

The water bottle belonging to Jose was orange.

5. Ⓨ Ⓝ

_____

6. Ⓨ Ⓝ

_____

4. Many plural nouns end in -*s* or -*es*. Which noun does **not** fit this rule?

___/6
Total

boat   ox   drink

5. Circle the adverb in the sentence.

Marco quietly slipped out of his bed.

6. Write a word that has the same -e*nd* spelling pattern as in *send*.

_____

NAME: _____ **DATE:** _____

DIRECTIONS Read and answer each question.

1. Write the name of a state.

_____

1. Ⓨ Ⓝ

2. Write the contraction to complete the sentence.

_____ you like to go after school?
(Where would)

2. Ⓨ Ⓝ

3. Ⓨ Ⓝ

3. Add commas to the letter.

Dear Pam
I saw you had a cast. I just wanted to check in
with you. How did you hurt your arm?
Your friend
Michael

4. Ⓨ Ⓝ

5. Ⓨ Ⓝ

6. Ⓨ Ⓝ

4. What would you call a large group of dogs?

| a swarm of dogs | a pack of dogs | a herd of dogs |

___ / 6
Total

5. Write the correct pronoun to complete the sentence.

How did you hurt_____?
(myself, herself, yourself)

6. Circle the word that is spelled correctly.

change   chanj   chanje

NAME: _____ DATE: _____

DIRECTIONS Read and answer each question.

1. (Y)(N)

2. (Y)(N)

3. (Y)(N)

4. (Y)(N)

5. (Y)(N)

6. (Y)(N)

___/6
Total

1. Which word is always capitalized?

Sincerely   A   Texas

2. Use an apostrophe to write *the leg of the table* in another way.

_____

3. Circle the correct greeting for a letter.

Dear Mr.   Dear Mr.   Dear, Mr.
Jackson;   Jackson,   Jackson

4. Write an adverb to complete the sentence.

The band played _____ for the crowd.

5. Complete the sentence with a noun and an adjective.

A bouquet of _____ is _____.

6. Circle the correctly spelled word.

ayr

airre

air

NAME: _____ **DATE:** _____

> **DIRECTIONS** Read and answer each question.

1. Which types of words are always capitalized?

proper nouns	long words	the last words in sentences

1. Ⓨ Ⓝ

2. Add apostrophes to the sentence.

The workers arent happy about work, so theyre going on strike.

2. Ⓨ Ⓝ

3. Ⓨ Ⓝ

3. Write the following as contractions.

we will	he is	you are
_____	_____	_____

4. Ⓨ Ⓝ

5. Ⓨ Ⓝ

4. Circle the adverb in the sentence.

The leaf fell softly from the tree.

6. Ⓨ Ⓝ

5. Circle the pronoun in the sentence.

The kids hid themselves in the forest.

___ / 6
Total

6. Write a word that has the same -*ch* ending as in *march*.

_____

NAME: _____ **DATE:** _____

DIRECTIONS Read and answer each question.

1. (Y)(N)

1. Circle the words that need capital letters.

Violet lives on david drive.

2. (Y)(N)

2. Rewrite the sentence with two contractions.

She is mad that he had been so mean to her.

3. (Y)(N)

_____

4. (Y)(N)

_____

5. (Y)(N)

3. Use an apostrophe to write *the zipper on the backpack* in another way.

6. (Y)(N)

_____

___/ 6
Total

4. Circle the adjectives in the sentence.

The small, blue bird chirped happily.

5. Write the plural noun to complete the sentence.

Lily's _____ were slightly wiggly.
        (tooth)

6. Write a word that has the same *-kn* spelling pattern as in *know*.

_____

NAME: _____ DATE: _____

DIRECTIONS Read and answer each question.

1. Circle the word that needs a capital letter.

The art teacher passed out the crayola® colored pencils.

1. Ⓨ Ⓝ

2. Circle the correct contraction.

couldve   couldh've   could've

2. Ⓨ Ⓝ

3. Ⓨ Ⓝ

3. Rewrite the sentence using an apostrophe.

The notebook belonging to Kai was missing.

_____

_____

4. Ⓨ Ⓝ

5. Ⓨ Ⓝ

6. Ⓨ Ⓝ

4. Many plural nouns end in *-s* or *-es*. Which noun does **not** fit this rule?

foot   napkin   shoe

___/6
Total

5. Circle the adverb in the sentence.

Nina usually walks to school with Fran.

6. Write a word that has the same *-ai* spelling pattern as in *rain*.

_____

NAME: _____ DATE: _____

SCORE

1. (Y)(N)

2. (Y)(N)

3. (Y)(N)

4. (Y)(N)

5. (Y)(N)

6. (Y)(N)

___ / 6
Total

DIRECTIONS Read and answer each question.

1. Circle the word that needs a capital letter.

My mom buys horizon® milk for our family.

2. Write the contraction to complete the sentence.

Tomatoes _____ vegetables. They are fruits.
(are not)

3. Add commas to the letter.

Dear Mom
I want a new book. Will you take me to the store?
Love
Luis

4. Complete the sentence with a noun and a verb.

A class of _____ went _____.

5. Circle the pronoun in the sentence.

Ava packed her suitcase for the sleepover.

6. Circle the word that is spelled correctly.

payd   payed   paid

NAME: _____ **DATE:** _____

DIRECTIONS Read and answer each question.

1. Circle the words that are always capitalized.

oregon   phone   mexico   twin lake

1. Ⓨ Ⓝ

2. Use an apostrophe to write *the pedal on the bike* in another way.

_____

2. Ⓨ Ⓝ

3. Ⓨ Ⓝ

3. Circle the correct greeting for a letter.

Dear Will,   Hello Will,   Will?

4. Ⓨ Ⓝ

4. Write an adverb to complete the sentence.

The musician played _____.

5. Ⓨ Ⓝ

6. Ⓨ Ⓝ

5. Complete the sentence with a noun and a verb.

A bunch of _____ were _____.

___/6
Total

6. Circle the correctly spelled word.

plase
place
plas

NAME: _____ DATE: _____

DIRECTIONS Read and answer each question.

1. Ⓨ Ⓝ

1. Circle the word that needs a capital letter.

I always choose the kellogg's® cereal to eat.

2. Ⓨ Ⓝ

2. Add apostrophes to the sentence.

Theyll be there when shes ready for them.

3. Ⓨ Ⓝ

3. Add apostrophes to the following contractions.

Im   theyll   mustve

4. Ⓨ Ⓝ

4. Circle the adverb in the sentence.

5. Ⓨ Ⓝ

The spider moved quickly to get to the web.

6. Ⓨ Ⓝ

5. Write the correct pronoun to complete the sentence.

___/6
Total

I can't hear _____ think when it is this
loud!   (myself, herself, yourself)

6. Write a word that has the same -*dge*
spelling pattern as in *edge*.

_____

NAME: _____ **DATE:** _____

| DIRECTIONS | Read and answer each question. |

1. Circle the words that need capital letters.

new hampshire is where my grandparents live.

1. Ⓨ Ⓝ

2. Rewrite the sentence with two contractions.

She is my best friend because she is kind and funny.

_____

_____

2. Ⓨ Ⓝ

3. Ⓨ Ⓝ

4. Ⓨ Ⓝ

3. Use an apostrophe to write *the ring belonging to Martha* in another way.

_____

5. Ⓨ Ⓝ

6. Ⓨ Ⓝ

4. Circle the adjectives in the sentence.

The big yellow school bus takes students to school.

___/ 6
Total

5. Circle the adverb in the sentence.

The woman drove safely with an infant in the back seat.

6. Write a word that has the same *-ing* spelling pattern as in *ring*.

_____

NAME: _____ DATE: _____

SCORE

1. (Y) (N)

2. (Y) (N)

3. (Y) (N)

4. (Y) (N)

5. (Y) (N)

6. (Y) (N)

___ / 6
Total

DIRECTIONS Read and answer each question.

1. Circle the word that needs a capital letter.

Our gym clothes at school are made by hanes®.

2. Circle the correct contraction.

whenwl'd   when'ld   when'd

3. Rewrite the sentence using an apostrophe.

The trampoline belonging to my neighbor was a lot of fun!

_____

_____

4. Many plural nouns end in *-s* or *-es*. Which noun does **not** fit this rule?

moose   broom   root

5. Circle the adverb in the sentence.

Some teachers rarely sit all day long.

6. Write a word that has the same *-ir* spelling pattern as in *shirt*.

_____

NAME: _____ **DATE:** _____

DIRECTIONS Read and answer each question.

1. Write the name of your street.

_____

1. Ⓨ Ⓝ

2. Circle the contraction in the sentence.

When's the best time to do your homework?

2. Ⓨ Ⓝ

3. Ⓨ Ⓝ

3. Add commas to the letter.

Dear Dad
I really need your help with my bike. I can't fix it.
Your son
Hector

4. Ⓨ Ⓝ

5. Ⓨ Ⓝ

6. Ⓨ Ⓝ

4. What would you call two shoes?

a pair of   a group of   a stack of
shoes   shoes   shoes

___ / 6
Total

5. Write the correct pronoun to complete the sentence.

I can make breakfast for_____.
(myself, herself, yourself)

6. Circle the word that is spelled correctly.

very   vairy   vayry

SCORE

1. Ⓨ Ⓝ

2. Ⓨ Ⓝ

3. Ⓨ Ⓝ

4. Ⓨ Ⓝ

5. Ⓨ Ⓝ

6. Ⓨ Ⓝ

___ / 6
Total

DIRECTIONS Read and answer each question.

1. Circle the words that need capital letters.

yesterday, mrs. dawes gave us too much homework.

2. Use an apostrophe to write *the keyboard on the computer* in another way.

_____

3. Circle the correct greeting for a letter.

To Shannon--   Hey Shannon!   Dear Shannon,

4. Write an adverb to complete the sentence.

The woman laughed _____ at her friend's joke.

5. Complete the sentence with a noun and an adjective.

A row of _____ was _____.

6. Circle the correctly spelled word.

lief

lyfe

life

NAME: _____ DATE: _____

DIRECTIONS Read and answer each question.

1. Circle the words that need capital letters.

do you want to play tennis
tonight, jesse?

2. Add apostrophes to the sentence.

The babys bottle is empty, so shes crying.

3. Add apostrophes to the following contractions.

whered   shes   theyll

4. Circle the adverb in the sentence.

The python slithered silently across the ground.

5. Write the correct pronoun to complete the sentence.

"Students, clean up after _____,"
said the teacher.   (ourselves, yourselves, yourself)

6. Write a word that has the same
-ou spelling pattern as in *loud*.

_____

1. Ⓨ Ⓝ

2. Ⓨ Ⓝ

3. Ⓨ Ⓝ

4. Ⓨ Ⓝ

5. Ⓨ Ⓝ

6. Ⓨ Ⓝ

___ / 6
Total

NAME: _____ **DATE:** _____

DIRECTIONS Read and answer each question.

1. Circle the words that need capital letters.

On halloween, we will be traveling to connecticut.

2. What kind of greeting would you write in a letter to your sibling?

_____

3. Rewrite the sentence using a contraction.

Dogs are not always friendly animals.

_____

_____

4. Circle the adjectives in the sentence.

I like to sit in the comfortable black chair in the living room.

5. Write a sentence using the plural noun *women*.

_____

_____

6. Circle the word that is spelled correctly.

cklump   klump   clump

NAME: _____ **DATE:** _____

DIRECTIONS Read and answer each question.

1. Why would you capitalize *Kentucky* in a sentence?

_____

1. Ⓨ Ⓝ

2. Circle the correct contraction.

shes   she's   shes'

2. Ⓨ Ⓝ

3. Ⓨ Ⓝ

3. Use an apostrophe to write *the tail of the mouse* in another way.

_____

4. Ⓨ Ⓝ

4. Many plural nouns end in *-s* or *-es*. Which noun does **not** fit this rule?

cup   deer   phone

5. Ⓨ Ⓝ

6. Ⓨ Ⓝ

5. Circle the adverbs in the sentence.

The sun shone brightly as I played happily at the park.

___/6
Total

6. Circle the correctly spelled word.

mouve

move

moove

NAME: _____ **DATE:** _____

DIRECTIONS Read and answer each question.

1. (Y)(N)

1. Why is *Easter* capitalized in a sentence?

_____

2. (Y)(N)

2. Circle the contraction in the sentence.

At my neighbor's house, they've got six chickens.

3. (Y)(N)

3. Write a closing for a letter to your pet.

_____

_____

4. (Y)(N)

4. What would you call a large number of puppies?

a flock   a team   a litter

5. (Y)(N)

5. Write the correct pronoun to complete the sentence.

6. (Y)(N)

"Keep your hands to_____,"
scolded Mom.   (myself, herself, yourself)

___/6
Total

6. Write a word that has the same *-old* ending as in *sold*.

_____

NAME: _____ **DATE:** _____

DIRECTIONS Read and answer each question.

1. Write a sentence about a holiday tradition.

_____

_____

1. Ⓨ Ⓝ

2. Use an apostrophe to write *the ears on Kira* another way.

_____

2. Ⓨ Ⓝ

3. Ⓨ Ⓝ

3. Add commas to the letter.

Dear Jeff
You are a great kid. I just need you to clean your room!
Love
Mom

4. Ⓨ Ⓝ

5. Ⓨ Ⓝ

6. Ⓨ Ⓝ

4. Write an adjective to complete the sentence.

The singer performed a _____ song.

___ / 6
Total

5. Write a verb to complete the sentence.

My friends can _____ all by themselves.

6. Circle the word that is spelled correctly.

great   grayt   grait

NAME: _____ DATE: _____

DIRECTIONS Read and answer each question.

1. Circle the words that need capital letters.

ned's favorite football team is from pittsburgh.

2. Add apostrophes to the sentence.

This soup isnt my favorite, but its actually pretty good!

3. Add apostrophes to the following contractions.

Im   didnt   well

4. What is the past tense of *ride*?

rided   roded   rode

5. Complete the sentence with a noun and an adjective.

A pile of _____ was found _____.

6. Circle the correctly spelled word.

towur

touwr

tower

NAME: _____ **DATE:** _____

DIRECTIONS Read and answer each question.

1. Circle the words that need capital letters.

Today, we head to columbia and durham.

1. Ⓨ Ⓝ

2. Write a greeting for a letter to your best friend.

_____

2. Ⓨ Ⓝ

3. Ⓨ Ⓝ

3. Rewrite the sentence with two contractions.

I would like to eat, but I cannot yet.

_____

_____

4. Ⓨ Ⓝ

5. Ⓨ Ⓝ

6. Ⓨ Ⓝ

4. Circle the adjectives in the sentence.

The rude man cut in line, and the angry customers complained.

___/6
Total

5. Rewrite the sentence in the past tense.

We swim in the pool for fun.

_____

_____

6. Write another word that has the same *-ink* spelling pattern as in *rink*.

_____

NAME: _____ **DATE:** _____

DIRECTIONS Read and answer each question.

1. (Y)(N)

1. Circle the word that needs a capital letter.

I prefer to buy the mead® brand of folders for my school work.

2. (Y)(N)

2. Circle the correct contraction.

howl'l howw'l how'll

3. (Y)(N)

3. Use an apostrophe to write *the bed in the hospital* in another way.

_____

4. (Y)(N)

4. Rewrite the sentence in the past tense.

I teach my friend how to play soccer.

_____

_____

5. (Y)(N)

6. (Y)(N)

___/6
Total

5. Circle the adverbs in the sentence.

The music played loudly while I lay quietly in my bed.

6. Write another word that has the same *-ing* spelling pattern as in *sing*.

_____

NAME: _____ **DATE:** _____

DIRECTIONS Read and answer each question.

SCORE

1. Circle the word that needs a capital letter.

Do you celebrate easter with your grandparents?

1. Ⓨ Ⓝ

2. Write the contraction to complete the sentence.

Third graders _____ be helpers in the cafeteria. (cannot)

2. Ⓨ Ⓝ

3. Ⓨ Ⓝ

3. Write a closing of a letter for your aunt.

_____

_____

4. Ⓨ Ⓝ

4. What would you call objects in straight lines?

bunches   rows   piles

5. Ⓨ Ⓝ

6. Ⓨ Ⓝ

5. Write the correct pronoun to complete the sentence.

The runners surprised _____ with their speed. (ourselves, themselves, yourselves)

___ / 6
Total

6. Write another word that has the same -ar spelling pattern as in harm.

_____

NAME: _____   **DATE:** _____

DIRECTIONS Read and answer each question.

1. Write the name of a place that always starts with a capital letter.

_____

2. Use an apostrophe to write *hair on my dog* in another way.

_____

3. Add commas to the letter.

Dear Steven
Your reading has improved
this year! I am very proud of you.
Your teacher
Mrs. Hanson

4. Write an adjective to complete the sentence.

The _____ book was hard to put down.

5. Complete the sentence with a noun and an adjective.

A bunch of _____ were _____.

6. Circle the word that is spelled correctly.

raile   rail   rayl

NAME: _____ **DATE:** _____

DIRECTIONS Read and answer each question.

1. Write the name of a city.

_____

1. Ⓨ Ⓝ

2. Write a greeting for the letter.

2. Ⓨ Ⓝ

_____

We loved our visit with you. You are such a great granddaughter. We miss you very much.

3. Ⓨ Ⓝ

3. Write a closing for the letter above.

4. Ⓨ Ⓝ

_____

_____

5. Ⓨ Ⓝ

4. Write a sentence about riding a bike using an adverb. Then, circle the adverb.

6. Ⓨ Ⓝ

_____

____ / 6
Total

_____

5. Write a sentence about the color of your eyes using an adjective. Then, circle the adjective.

_____

_____

6. Circle the word that is spelled correctly.

greet   greit   greyt

NAME: _____ **DATE:** _____

SCORE

DIRECTIONS Read and answer each question.

1. Y N

2. Y N

3. Y N

4. Y N

5. Y N

6. Y N

___ / 6
Total

1. Circle the words that need capital letters.

Mariela had to prepare for a valentine's day party.

2. Write a greeting for the letter.

_____

You did a great job at the game! I loved watching you get your trophy. I am very proud of you.

3. Write a closing for the letter above.

_____

_____

4. Circle the adjectives in the sentence.

The fluffy pillow felt comfortable against my head.

5. Write a sentence using the plural noun *teeth*.

_____

_____

6. Circle the correctly spelled word.

book
boock
boowk

NAME: _____ DATE: _____

DIRECTIONS Read and answer each question.

1. Why is *Nature Valley*® capitalized in a sentence?

_____

1. Ⓨ Ⓝ

2. Circle the correct contraction.

hadn't   had'nt   hadnt'

2. Ⓨ Ⓝ

3. Ⓨ Ⓝ

3. Use an apostrophe to write *the hairband belonging to Maria* in another way.

_____

4. Ⓨ Ⓝ

4. Many plural nouns end in *-s* or *-es*. Which noun does **not** fit this rule?

hand   rug   foot

5. Ⓨ Ⓝ

5. Circle the adverbs in the sentence.

Tina loudly screamed at her mom, who was blindly crossing in front of a car.

6. Ⓨ Ⓝ

___ / 6
Total

6. Circle the correctly spelled word.

kewl
cool
kowl

© Shell Education

NAME: _____ **DATE:** _____

DIRECTIONS   Read and answer each question.

1.   Circle the word that needs a capital letter.

Mom will decide how long we can play with our nintendo® game.

2.   Write the contraction to complete the sentence.

_____ not how I like my friends to treat me.
(That is)

3.   Write a closing for a letter to a newspaper editor.

_____

_____

4.   What would you call a large group of judges?

an army   a crowd   a panel

5.   Write the correct pronoun to complete the sentence.

"What will I do with _____ today?"
Ana wondered.   (myself, herself, yourself)

6.   Circle the word that has the same -*oo* spelling pattern, as in *book*.

took

loot

root

NAME: _____ **DATE:** _____

DIRECTIONS   Read and answer each question.

1. Circle the words that need capital letters.

The time between thanksgiving and christmas goes by very quickly.

2. Use an apostrophe to write *the sister of Russ* in another way.

_____

3. Add commas to the letter.

Dear Mom
Thank you for being a wonderful mom.
Love
Amanda

4. Write an adjective to complete the sentence.

Our _____ pet chewed Dad's shoes again.

5. Complete the sentence with a verb and a noun.

I can _____ in a bunch of _____.

6. Circle the word that is spelled correctly.

touch   toutch   tutch

1. Ⓨ Ⓝ

2. Ⓨ Ⓝ

3. Ⓨ Ⓝ

4. Ⓨ Ⓝ

5. Ⓨ Ⓝ

6. Ⓨ Ⓝ

___ / 6
Total

NAME: _____ **DATE:** _____

SCORE

1. Y N

2. Y N

3. Y N

4. Y N

5. Y N

6. Y N

___/ 6
Total

DIRECTIONS Read and answer each question.

1. Circle the words that need capital letters.

Are you rooting for the team from texas or arkansas?

2. Add apostrophes to the sentence.

She wont take medicine unless its mixed with something.

3. Add apostrophes to the following contractions.

Im   cant   shed

4. Circle the adverb in the sentence.

The sisters swam happily together.

5. Complete the sentence with a plural noun.

_____ come in a set.

6. Circle the word that is spelled correctly.

owr   our   ouer

NAME: _____ **DATE:** _____

DIRECTIONS Read and answer each question.

1. Circle the words that need capital letters.

The bus will stop in brighton, newberg, and warren.

1. Ⓨ Ⓝ

2. Write a greeting for a letter to a family member.

_____

2. Ⓨ Ⓝ

3. Rewrite the sentence with two contractions.

I would like to go home, but I will stay longer.

_____

_____

3. Ⓨ Ⓝ

4. Ⓨ Ⓝ

4. Circle the adjectives in the sentence.

The small bird flapped its blue wings and flew away.

5. Ⓨ Ⓝ

6. Ⓨ Ⓝ

5. Rewrite the sentence in the past tense.

I tear the paper for my art project.

_____

_____

___ / 6

Total

6. Write another word that has the same -ink spelling pattern as in link.

_____

NAME: _____ **DATE:** _____

SCORE

DIRECTIONS Read and answer each question.

1. (Y) (N)

1. Circle the word that needs a capital letter.

Can we go to the apple® store and buy a new part for our computer?

2. (Y) (N)

2. Circle the correct contraction.

3. (Y) (N)

mighthv'e   mighth've   might've

4. (Y) (N)

3. Use an apostrophe to write *the fur on the dog* in another way.

5. (Y) (N)

_____

6. (Y) (N)

4. Rewrite the sentence in the past tense.

I wake in the morning when the sun comes up.

___/ 6
Total

_____

_____

5. Circle the adverbs in the sentence.

The phone rang loudly, so I jumped up suddenly.

6. Write another word that has the same *-ing* spelling pattern as in *bring*.

_____

NAME: _____ **DATE:** _____

DIRECTIONS Read and answer each question.

1. Circle the words that need capital letters.

How do you celebrate martin luther king jr.'s birthday?

2. Write the contraction to complete the sentence.

Bullying _____ tolerated at school.

(is not)

3. Write a closing in a letter to a grandparent.

_____

_____

4. Write a sentence using the word *school* to describe a group of animals.

_____

_____

5. Write the correct pronoun to complete the sentence.

My friend and I were hungry, so we helped _____ to a snack.
(ourselves, themselves, yourselves)

6. Write another word that has the same *-ar* spelling pattern as in *dart*.

_____

1. Ⓨ Ⓝ

2. Ⓨ Ⓝ

3. Ⓨ Ⓝ

4. Ⓨ Ⓝ

5. Ⓨ Ⓝ

6. Ⓨ Ⓝ

___ / 6
Total

NAME: _____ DATE: _____

SCORE

1. Ⓨ Ⓝ

2. Ⓨ Ⓝ

3. Ⓨ Ⓝ

4. Ⓨ Ⓝ

5. Ⓨ Ⓝ

6. Ⓨ Ⓝ

___ / 6
Total

DIRECTIONS Read and answer each question.

1. Circle the words that need capital letters.

our family is going out of town in august.

2. Use an apostrophe to write *mane of a horse* in another way.

_____

3. Add commas to the letter.

Dear Hank
I am sorry I hurt your feelings. Please forgive me.
Your neighbor
Joe

4. Write an adjective to complete the sentence.

The swimming pool is fun on a _____ day.

5. Complete the sentence with a noun and an adjective.

A series of _____ were _____.

6. Circle the correctly spelled word.

haile
hail
hayl

NAME: _____ **DATE:** _____

DIRECTIONS Read and answer each question.

1. Write the name of a holiday.

_____

1. Ⓨ Ⓝ

2. Write a greeting for the letter.

2. Ⓨ Ⓝ

_____

What time is the game? I will be there a few
minutes early. I can't wait to watch you play.

3. Ⓨ Ⓝ

3. Write a closing for the letter above.

4. Ⓨ Ⓝ

_____

_____

5. Ⓨ Ⓝ

4. Write a sentence about how you ate your lunch
using an adverb.

6. Ⓨ Ⓝ

_____

_____

___ / 6
Total

5. Write a sentence about the weather today using
an adjective.

_____

_____

6. Circle the word that is spelled correctly.

seet   seit   seat

NAME: _____ **DATE:** _____

SCORE

1. Ⓨ Ⓝ

2. Ⓨ Ⓝ

3. Ⓨ Ⓝ

4. Ⓨ Ⓝ

5. Ⓨ Ⓝ

6. Ⓨ Ⓝ

___ / 6
Total

DIRECTIONS Read and answer each question.

1. Circle the word that needs a capital letter.

i can't believe it is almost spring break.

2. Add an apostrophe to the sentence.

My brothers friend has a great game called *Baseball Fan*.

3. Write the words that make up each contraction.

that's   can't

_____   _____

4. Write an adjective to complete the sentence.

The _____ soup was too hot to eat.

5. What is the past tense of write?

writing   wrote   write

6. Circle the word that is spelled correctly.

ranj   ranje   range

NAME: _____ **DATE:** _____

DIRECTIONS Read and answer each question.

1. Circle the word that needs a capital letter.

The art teacher shows the students how to use the elmer's® glue carefully.

2. Circle the correct contraction.

would've   wouldh've   would'hve

3. Write a sentence about *a game belonging to a friend.* Use an apostrophe.

_____

_____

4. Write an adverb to complete the sentence.

Logan skateboarded _____ and then got hurt.

5. Circle the adjectives in the sentence.

Wes has red hair, and it makes him look unique.

6. Circle the word that is spelled correctly.

rinsce   rince   rinse

1. Ⓨ Ⓝ

2. Ⓨ Ⓝ

3. Ⓨ Ⓝ

4. Ⓨ Ⓝ

5. Ⓨ Ⓝ

6. Ⓨ Ⓝ

___/6
Total

NAME: _____ **DATE:** _____

DIRECTIONS Read and answer each question.

1. Ⓨ Ⓝ

1. Write a sentence about a brand your family buys using correct capitalization.

_____

_____

2. Ⓨ Ⓝ

3. Ⓨ Ⓝ

2. Circle the contraction in the sentence.

Why won't the group start getting its work done?

4. Ⓨ Ⓝ

3. Add commas to the letter.

5. Ⓨ Ⓝ

Dear dentist
I am nervous to see you. I have not been flossing like you told me to.
Your patient
Ella

6. Ⓨ Ⓝ

___ / 6
Total

4. What would you call a lot of bananas?

| a chain of bananas | a bunch of bananas | a pile of bananas |

5. Circle the pronoun in the sentence.

After a lot of practice, Claire could swim in the deep end by herself.

6. Circle the word that is spelled correctly.

| balans | balance | balanse |

NAME: _____ **DATE:** _____

DIRECTIONS Read and answer each question.

1. Which word is always capitalized?

Vacation   Utah   To

1. Ⓨ Ⓝ

2. What is another way to write *the mother of your friend*?

_____

2. Ⓨ Ⓝ

3. Ⓨ Ⓝ

3. Add commas to the letter.

Dear Dad
I am sorry you broke your leg. May I sign your cast?
Your daughter
Alice

4. Ⓨ Ⓝ

5. Ⓨ Ⓝ

6. Ⓨ Ⓝ

4. Write an adverb to complete the sentence.

Max yelled _____ so that his friends could hear him.

___/6
Total

5. What is the past tense of *make*?

maked   maken   made

6. Circle the word that is spelled correctly.

pitty   pity   pitey

NAME: _____ DATE: _____

SCORE

DIRECTIONS Read and answer each question.

1. Which types of words are always capitalized?

1. Ⓨ Ⓝ

adjectives   continent names   food names

2. Ⓨ Ⓝ

2. Add apostrophes to the sentence.

Gus wasnt sure that the pools heater was turned on because the water was cold.

3. Ⓨ Ⓝ

3. Add apostrophes to the following contractions.

4. Ⓨ Ⓝ

whats   mightnt   Ive

5. Ⓨ Ⓝ

4. Circle the adverb in the sentence.

6. Ⓨ Ⓝ

Sophie ran out on the soccer field quickly so that she had time to practice.

___ / 6
Total

5. Write the past tense word to complete the sentence.

The boss _____ his workers once a month.
                  (pays)

6. Circle the word that is spelled correctly.

page   paje   padg

NAME: _____ **DATE:** _____

DIRECTIONS Read and answer each question.

1. Circle the words that need capital letters.

The states of north carolina and south carolina border each other.

1. Ⓨ Ⓝ

2. Ⓨ Ⓝ

2. What is the proper way to greet your mother in a letter?

Mom?   Dear Mom,   Hi Mom!

3. Ⓨ Ⓝ

3. Circle the contractions in the sentence.

Air pollution isn't always visible, but it's still all around us.

4. Ⓨ Ⓝ

5. Ⓨ Ⓝ

4. Circle the adjectives in the sentence.

The brown bear walked along the icy river, looking for fresh salmon to eat.

6. Ⓨ Ⓝ

___ / 6
Total

5. Write the plural noun to complete the sentence.

I don't know if the _____ work at the library.
          (woman)

6. Circle the word that is spelled correctly.

heal   heeal   hele

NAME: _____   DATE: _____

SCORE

DIRECTIONS Read and answer each question.

1. $\boxed{Y}$ $\boxed{N}$

1. Why do you capitalize *Christmas* in a sentence?

_____

2. $\boxed{Y}$ $\boxed{N}$

2. Circle the correct contraction.

whyh'd   why'd   why'hd

3. $\boxed{Y}$ $\boxed{N}$

3. Use an apostrophe to write *the garden at our school* in another way.

4. $\boxed{Y}$ $\boxed{N}$

_____

5. $\boxed{Y}$ $\boxed{N}$

4. Many plural nouns end in -*s* or -*es*. Which noun does **not** follow this rule?

6. $\boxed{Y}$ $\boxed{N}$

fire   flame   wool

___/6
Total

5. Circle the adverb in the sentence.

Who can ride a scooter quickly without getting hurt?

6. Circle the correctly spelled word.

preecher
preacher
precher

NAME: _____ DATE: _____

DIRECTIONS Read and answer each question.

1. Write a sentence about a brand of ice cream you eat using correct capitalization.

_____

_____

1. Ⓨ Ⓝ

2. Ⓨ Ⓝ

2. Circle the contraction in the sentence.

The teacher should've warned us that we were having a test so we could have studied.

3. Ⓨ Ⓝ

4. Ⓨ Ⓝ

3. Add apostrophes to the following contractions.

Ill   couldnt   heres

5. Ⓨ Ⓝ

4. What would you call a large number of teachers?

| a faculty of teachers | an army of teachers | a swarm of teachers |

6. Ⓨ Ⓝ

___ / 6
Total

5. Write the correct pronoun to complete the sentence.

You are not allowed to have _____ as a secret buddy.   (yourself, ourselves)

6. Circle the word that is spelled correctly.

stitch   stich   stijch

NAME: _____ DATE: _____

SCORE

DIRECTIONS Read and answer each question.

1. Ⓨ Ⓝ

1. Circle the words that need capital letters.

I wanted to wake up early and make breakfast for my mom the morning of mother's day.

2. Ⓨ Ⓝ

2. Add an apostrophe to one of the sentences.

My friends so nice. I am lucky to know her.

3. Ⓨ Ⓝ

3. Write the words that make up each contraction.

we'd   let's

_____   _____

4. Ⓨ Ⓝ

4. Write two adjectives about homework.

_____   _____

5. Ⓨ Ⓝ

5. Complete the sentence with two nouns.

A swarm of _____ moved _____.

6. Ⓨ Ⓝ

___/6
Total

6. Circle the correctly spelled word.

took
touk
towk

NAME: _____ **DATE:** _____

DIRECTIONS Read and answer each question.

1. Circle the words that need capital letters.

central america is directly north of south america.

1. Ⓨ Ⓝ

2. Add apostrophes to the sentence.

The dog park isnt open because the parks gates are broken and dogs might escape.

2. Ⓨ Ⓝ

3. Ⓨ Ⓝ

3. Rewrite the following words as contractions.

could not   might have

_____   _____

4. Ⓨ Ⓝ

5. Ⓨ Ⓝ

4. Write two adjectives about cafeteria food.

_____   _____

6. Ⓨ Ⓝ

___ / 6
Total

5. Write a plural noun to complete the sentence

The herd of _____ roamed the land in search of food.

6. Circle the correctly spelled word.

wayd
wade
waid

NAME: _____ DATE: _____

DIRECTIONS Read and answer each question.

1. (Y)(N)

1. Write a sentence about a place you would like to go on vacation.

_____

2. (Y)(N)

_____

3. (Y)(N)

2. Add punctuation to the letter greeting.

Dear Mom and Dad

4. (Y)(N)

3. Write the contraction to complete the sentence.

5. (Y)(N)

The rain _____ stop so let's go inside.
        (will not)

6. (Y)(N)

4. Write a noun to complete the sentence.

___/6
Total

The bright _____ attracted all the bees.

5. What is the past tense of *catch*?

catched   catchy   caught

6. Circle the correctly spelled word.

ranj
ranje
range

NAME: _____ **DATE:** _____

DIRECTIONS Read and answer each question.

1. Circle the words that need capital letters.

whenever I have a cold, I sleep with a kleenex™ box next to my bed.

2. What are the two meanings of *how's*?

how's = _____

how's = _____

3. Write an object that belongs to your classmate.

_____'s _____

4. Circle the adverb to complete the sentence.

The car sped quickly down the road.

5. Circle the adjectives in the sentence.

The tall woman has beautiful, long hair.

6. Circle the word that is spelled correctly.

koff   coff   cough

1. Ⓨ Ⓝ

2. Ⓨ Ⓝ

3. Ⓨ Ⓝ

4. Ⓨ Ⓝ

5. Ⓨ Ⓝ

6. Ⓨ Ⓝ

___ / 6
Total

NAME: _____ DATE: _____

DIRECTIONS Read and answer each question.

1. Name a continent.

_____

2. Circle the contractions in the sentence.

The artwork can't fit on the wall because it's too big.

3. Write an object that belongs to a family member.

_____'s _____

4. Write the correct verb to complete the sentence.

The baby piglet had _____ his mother and cuddled with her.   (find, found)

5. Circle the pronoun in the sentence.

The ant can carry huge, heavy objects by itself.

6. Circle the correctly spelled word.

happines
happiness
happinness

NAME: _____   **DATE:** _____

DIRECTIONS   Read and answer each question.

1. Which word is always capitalized?

Me   Vermont   Vacation

1. Ⓨ Ⓝ

2. What is another way to write *the pencil belongs to Sheila*?

Sheila's pencil   Sheilas' pencil   Sheilas pencil

2. Ⓨ Ⓝ

3. Ⓨ Ⓝ

3. Write a short letter with one or two sentences. Don't forget the greeting and closing.

_____

_____

_____

_____

4. Ⓨ Ⓝ

5. Ⓨ Ⓝ

6. Ⓨ Ⓝ

___ / 6
Total

4. Write an adverb to complete the sentence.

The clown juggled the balls _____
during the circus performance.

5. What is the past tense of *pay*?

paide   payd   paid

6. Circle the word that is spelled correctly.

confusion   confushun   confution

NAME: _____ DATE: _____

DIRECTIONS Read and answer each question.

1. Write an example of a brand name you know.

_____

2. Add an apostrophe to the sentence.

The seal shouldve watched out more carefully for those killer whales.

3. Write contractions for the following phrases.

who will   there is

_____   _____

4. Circle the adverb in the sentence.

The students busily put away their backpacks to start their day.

5. Write the past tense word to complete the sentence.

Yesterday I _____ to get my bag, but I forgot it.
(mean)

6. Circle the word that is spelled correctly.

addishun   addision   addition

NAME: _____ **DATE:** _____

DIRECTIONS Read and answer each question.

1. Circle the word that needs a capital letter.

Should we go to hawaii for summer vacation?

1. Ⓨ Ⓝ

2. Ⓨ Ⓝ

2. Write the two meanings of *why's*.

why's = _____

why's = _____

3. Ⓨ Ⓝ

3. Write a closing to a letter for a doctor.

_____

_____

4. Ⓨ Ⓝ

5. Ⓨ Ⓝ

4. Circle the adjectives in the sentence.

The prickly cactus bloomed and is covered with red flowers.

6. Ⓨ Ⓝ

___/ 6
Total

5. Circle the plural noun in the sentence.

Would the men be able to check the engine on my car?

6. Circle the word that is spelled correctly.

thoughtfull   thoughfel   thoughtful

NAME: _____ **DATE:** _____

SCORE

1. Ⓨ Ⓝ

2. Ⓨ Ⓝ

3. Ⓨ Ⓝ

4. Ⓨ Ⓝ

5. Ⓨ Ⓝ

6. Ⓨ Ⓝ

___ / 6
Total

DIRECTIONS Read and answer each question.

1. Circle the words that need capital letters.

Did you know that the capital of italy is rome or that the capital of germany is berlin?

2. Write a short thank-you note to a friend. Include commas in your greeting and closing.

_____

_____

_____

_____

3. Use an apostrophe to write *the horns of the bull* in another way.

_____

4. Many plural nouns end in *-s* or *-es*. Which noun does **not** follow this rule?

sheep   bear   lion

5. Circle the adverb in the sentence.

The kitten playfully swatted the ball of yarn.

6. Circle the word that is spelled correctly.

brightness   briteness   britenes

NAME: _____ **DATE:** _____

DIRECTIONS Read and answer each question.

1. Write a sentence about a brand of toys you play with using correct capitalization.

_____

_____

2. Write the contraction to complete the sentence.

I hope that _____ learned an important
                   (you have)

lesson about being a good friend.

3. Add apostrophes to the following contractions.

weve   shell   whod

4. What would you call a large group of people watching a performance?

a host   a panel   an audience

5. Write a verb to complete the sentence.

We could not _____ ourselves.

6. Circle the word that is spelled correctly.

direcsion   direction   direcshun

1. Ⓨ Ⓝ

2. Ⓨ Ⓝ

3. Ⓨ Ⓝ

4. Ⓨ Ⓝ

5. Ⓨ Ⓝ

6. Ⓨ Ⓝ

___/6
Total

NAME: _____ **DATE:** _____

DIRECTIONS Read and answer each question.

1. Which is always capitalized?

New Year's Day   To   From

2. Use an apostrophe to write *the icicle from the house* in another way.

_____

3. Write a short note to your teacher. Include commas in your greeting and closing.

_____

_____

_____

_____

4. Write two adjectives about celebrating a birthday.

_____   _____

5. Complete the sentence with a verb.

I don't like to _____ all by myself.

6. Circle the word that is spelled correctly.

britist   brightist   brightest

NAME: _____ DATE: _____

DIRECTIONS Read and answer each question.

1. Circle the words that need capital letters.

Some people decided to travel to omaha, while others headed the other way, to topeka.

2. Add apostrophes to the sentence.

Kevins aunt isnt the nicest person in the world.

3. Rewrite the following words as contractions.

do not   will not

_____   _____

4. Circle the adverb in the sentence.

We visited Grandpa in the hospital and cheerfully told him to feel better.

5. Write a noun to complete the sentence.

A crowd of _____ approached us outside of school.

6. Circle the word that is spelled correctly.

selekt   seleckt   select

NAME: _____ **DATE:** _____

DIRECTIONS Read and answer each question.

1. Write a sentence about the city you live in.

_____

_____

2. Write the two meanings of *they'd*.

they'd = _____

they'd = _____

3. Circle the contractions in the sentence.

The librarian must've set the book aside for me because I don't see it here.

4. What would you call a large group of judges?

a host   a panel   an audience

5. What is the past tense of *write*?

wrate   wrote   writing

6. Circle the word that is spelled correctly.

exchanj   exchanje   exchange

NAME: _____ **DATE:** _____

DIRECTIONS Read and answer each question.

1. Circle the words that need capital letters.

Our family loves to watch fireworks on the fourth of july.

2. Add apostrophes to the contractions below.

arent   its   wasnt

3. Write the words that make up each contraction.

what's   isn't

_____   _____

4. Write an adjective to complete the sentence.

I noticed the _____ bike right away when I walked in the store.

5. Circle the adjectives in the sentence.

The new computer was quite a nice surprise.

6. Circle the word that is spelled correctly.

determine   determin   detourmine

NAME: _____ **DATE:** _____

DIRECTIONS Read and answer each question.

1. Write a sentence about a product you have seen at the grocery store using correct capitalization.

_____

_____

2. Circle the contraction in the sentence.

The principal wouldn't tell us which class won the pizza party until the end of the day.

3. Add commas to the letter.

Dear Mason
You are working hard. Keep it up!
Sincerely
Principal Jefferson

4. What would you call a group of musicians?

a band   a team   a faculty

5. Complete the sentence with a verb.

I cannot wait to _____ all by myself.

6. Circle the word that is spelled correctly.

represent   reprecent   represent

NAME: _____ DATE: _____

DIRECTIONS Read and answer each question.

1. Circle the words that should always be capitalized.

Washington   Mom   Halloween

2. What is another way to write *the robot belonging to Noah*?

Noahs robot's   Noahs' robot   Noah's robot

3. What is another way to write *the time machine belonging to the scientist*?

_____

4. What would you call a group of tools?

a band   a team   a set

5. What is the past tense of *sting*?

stang   stung   stinged

6. Circle the correctly spelled word.

geometric
geeohmetrick
geometrick

1. Ⓨ Ⓝ

2. Ⓨ Ⓝ

3. Ⓨ Ⓝ

4. Ⓨ Ⓝ

5. Ⓨ Ⓝ

6. Ⓨ Ⓝ

___ / 6
Total

NAME: _____ DATE: _____

DIRECTIONS Read and answer each question.

SCORE

1. Ⓨ Ⓝ

2. Ⓨ Ⓝ

3. Ⓨ Ⓝ

4. Ⓨ Ⓝ

5. Ⓨ Ⓝ

6. Ⓨ Ⓝ

___/ 6
Total

1. Circle the word that needs a capital letter.

jayden's family was very excited. They were together for a party.

2. Add an apostrophe.

"A new video game! Its exactly what I wanted," yelled Scott.

3. Write the words that make up each contraction.

couldn't   it's

_____   _____

4. Circle the adverb in the sentence.

Olivia cleaned her dirty room promptly before her friends saw it.

5. Circle the adjectives in the sentence.

Olivia cleaned her dirty room promptly before her close friends saw it.

6. Circle the word that is spelled correctly.

grateful   greatfull   greatful

NAME: _____ **DATE:** _____

DIRECTIONS Read and answer each question.

1. Circle the words that need capital letters.

The capital of china is beijing.

1. Ⓨ Ⓝ

2. What is the proper way to greet someone in a letter?

Dear Aiden,   What's up?   Hey there!

2. Ⓨ Ⓝ

3. Ⓨ Ⓝ

3. Circle the contraction in the sentence.

The storm caused us to lose power, so we couldn't watch television.

4. Ⓨ Ⓝ

4. Circle the adjectives in the sentence.

The slimy monster had eight heads and red eyes.

5. Ⓨ Ⓝ

6. Ⓨ Ⓝ

5. Write the plural noun to complete the sentence.

I saw _____ in the basement.
            (mouse)

___ / 6
Total

6. Circle the word that is spelled correctly.

sphear   sphere   sfere

NAME: _____   DATE: _____

SCORE

1. Ⓨ Ⓝ

2. Ⓨ Ⓝ

3. Ⓨ Ⓝ

4. Ⓨ Ⓝ

5. Ⓨ Ⓝ

6. Ⓨ Ⓝ

___ / 6
Total

DIRECTIONS Read and answer each question.

1. Circle the words that need capital letters.

I'd love to travel to asia to see japan, china, thailand, and the philippines.

2. Add apostrophes to the contractions.

cant   weve   shouldnt

3. Use an apostrophe to write *the tiara on the princess* in another way.

_____

4. Many plural nouns end in *-s* or *-es*. Which noun does **not** follow this rule?

sea   bison   water

5. Circle the adverb in the sentence.

The puppy playfully nipped at the chew toy.

6. Circle the correctly spelled word.

hapines

happiness

happyness

NAME: _____ **DATE:** _____

| DIRECTIONS | Read and answer each question. |

1. Write a sentence about the brand of shoes you are wearing using correct capitalization.

_____

_____

2. Circle the contraction in the sentence.

We go to my grandparents' house a lot, and they're always happy to see us.

3. Add apostrophes to the following contractions.

whered   hows   whos

4. What is a *choir*?

A choir is a group of _____ that

_____ .

5. Circle the pronouns in the sentence.

Our class cannot wait to show ourselves off in our costumes for the play.

6. Circle the word that is spelled correctly.

second   seckond   sekond

1. Ⓨ Ⓝ

2. Ⓨ Ⓝ

3. Ⓨ Ⓝ

4. Ⓨ Ⓝ

5. Ⓨ Ⓝ

6. Ⓨ Ⓝ

___/6
Total

NAME: _____ **DATE:** _____

SCORE

1. Ⓨ Ⓝ

2. Ⓨ Ⓝ

3. Ⓨ Ⓝ

4. Ⓨ Ⓝ

5. Ⓨ Ⓝ

6. Ⓨ Ⓝ

___ / 6
Total

DIRECTIONS Read and answer each question.

1. Which items are **not** capitalized?

brand names   holidays   ice cream flavors

2. Use an apostrophe to write *the scarf that Fiona is wearing* in another way.

_____

3. Write a short note to a classmate. Include commas in the greeting and closing.

_____

_____

_____

_____

4. Write two adjectives about winter.

_____   _____

5. Complete the sentence with two nouns.

There was a pile of _____ on the

_____ .

6. Circle the word that is spelled correctly.

dreemer   dreimer   dreamer

NAME: _____   **DATE:** _____

DIRECTIONS Read and answer each question.

1. Circle the words that need capital letters.

Would you like to see pictures from our trip to indonesia and vietnam?

2. Add apostrophes to the sentence.

The neighbors house is very scary, so we cant go in it alone.

3. Rewrite the following words as contractions.

should not   would have

_____   _____

4. Write two adjectives about how people swim.

_____   _____

5. Write a noun to complete the sentence.

The basket of _____ sat on the counter.

6. Circle the word that is spelled correctly.

reeson

reason

reasin

1. Ⓨ Ⓝ

2. Ⓨ Ⓝ

3. Ⓨ Ⓝ

4. Ⓨ Ⓝ

5. Ⓨ Ⓝ

6. Ⓨ Ⓝ

___ / 6
Total

NAME: _____ **DATE:** _____

DIRECTIONS Read and answer each question.

1. (Y)(N)

1. Write a sentence about a special place you would like to live. Be sure to use correct capitalization.

_____

2. (Y)(N)

_____

3. (Y)(N)

2. Add punctuation to the letter greeting.

Dear Professor Stevens

4. (Y)(N)

3. Rewrite the sentence with a contraction.

The baby did not like to be in the crib alone.

5. (Y)(N)

_____

6. (Y)(N)

_____

___ / 6
Total

4. Write an adverb to complete the sentence.

The group hiked _____ up the mountain.

5. What is the past tense of *find*?

finded   finding   found

6. Circle the word that is spelled correctly.

chandge   chanje   change

NAME: _____ DATE: _____

DIRECTIONS Read and answer each question.

1. Circle the words that need capital letters.

The store sold a lot of school supplies, including crayola® markers and bic® ballpoint pens.

2. Write the words that make up the following contractions.

would've   could've

_____   _____

3. Use an apostrophe to write *the new jeans that belong to Christina* in another way.

_____

4. Write an adverb to complete the sentence.

The little girl read the book _____ because she was so interested in the story.

5. Circle the adjectives in the sentence.

The bright light kept us up through the long night.

6. Circle the word that is spelled correctly.

direcshun   direcktion   direction

1. Ⓨ Ⓝ

2. Ⓨ Ⓝ

3. Ⓨ Ⓝ

4. Ⓨ Ⓝ

5. Ⓨ Ⓝ

6. Ⓨ Ⓝ

___ / 6
Total

NAME: _____ DATE: _____

DIRECTIONS Read and answer each question.

1. Why is *John* always capitalized in a sentence?

_____

2. Write a sentence about something you *cannot* do using a contraction.

_____

_____

3. Write the words that make up the contractions.

haven't   weren't

_____   _____

4. Write two adjectives about summer vacation.

_____   _____

5. Write the correct pronoun to complete the sentence.

My younger sister is still learning how to walk all by

_____.

(yourself, her, herself)

6. Circle the word that is spelled correctly.

revize   revice   revise

NAME: _____ **DATE:** _____

DIRECTIONS Read and answer each question.

1. Which word should **not** be capitalized?

Ohio   Boston   Location   Jacksonville

1. Ⓨ Ⓝ

2. What is another way to write *the spark from the fire*?

_____

2. Ⓨ Ⓝ

3. Ⓨ Ⓝ

3. Write a sentence about something you *should have* done using a contraction.

_____

_____

4. Ⓨ Ⓝ

5. Ⓨ Ⓝ

4. Write an adverb to complete the sentence.

The spaceship departed _____ from the landing strip.

6. Ⓨ Ⓝ

___ / 6
Total

5. What is the past tense of *get*?

getted   got   getting

6. Write a word that includes the -*ness* spelling pattern as in *goodness*.

_____

NAME: _____ **DATE:** _____

SCORE

1. Ⓨ Ⓝ

2. Ⓨ Ⓝ

3. Ⓨ Ⓝ

4. Ⓨ Ⓝ

5. Ⓨ Ⓝ

6. Ⓨ Ⓝ

___ / 6
Total

DIRECTIONS Read and answer each question.

1. Write your teacher's name using correct capitalization.

_____

2. Write two possessive nouns.

_____'s   _____'s

3. Write two contractions.

_____   _____

4. Circle the adverb in the sentence.

The clock ticked continually throughout the day.

5. Write the past tense form of *hear* to complete the sentence.

I _____ the playground rules have changed.

6. Write a word that includes the *-tion* spelling pattern as in *destination*.

_____

NAME: _____ **DATE:** _____

DIRECTIONS Read and answer each question.

1. Circle the words that need capital letters.

The country of haiti is part of an island in the caribbean.

2. Write about something you *might have* done using a contraction.

_____

_____

3. Write the words that make up the contractions.

haven't   hadn't

_____   _____

4. Write two adjectives about recess.

_____   _____

5. Complete the sentence with two nouns.

I may see a group of _____ on a

_____.

6. Write a word that includes the -sion spelling pattern as in *decision*.

_____

1. Ⓨ Ⓝ

2. Ⓨ Ⓝ

3. Ⓨ Ⓝ

4. Ⓨ Ⓝ

5. Ⓨ Ⓝ

6. Ⓨ Ⓝ

___ / 6
Total

NAME: _____ DATE: _____

DIRECTIONS Read and answer each question.

1. Circle the days that should always be capitalized.

Memorial Day   Thanksgiving   Yesterday

2. Write the following as contractions.

I am   she is

_____   _____

3. Use an apostrophe to write *the toothbrush belonging to Lucas* in another way.

_____

4. Write two adjectives about your best friend.

_____   _____

5. Complete the sentence with two nouns.

I may see a team of _____ at a

_____.

6. Write a word that includes the *-ful* spelling pattern as in *beautiful*.

_____

NAME: _____ **DATE:** _____

DIRECTIONS Read and answer each question.

1. Write the name of the place where you were born using correct capitalization.

_____

1. Ⓨ Ⓝ

2. Write the contraction to complete the sentence.

The cafeteria _____ served something special. (must have)

2. Ⓨ Ⓝ

3. Ⓨ Ⓝ

3. Add apostrophes to the following contractions.

Ill   couldnt   wouldve

4. Ⓨ Ⓝ

5. Ⓨ Ⓝ

4. What would you call a large amount of cows?

a herd of cows   a class of cows   a pack of cows

6. Ⓨ Ⓝ

5. Write the correct pronoun to complete the sentence.

We must protect _____ by (yourselves, themselves, ourselves)

always wearing bike helmets while riding.

___ / 6
Total

6. Circle the word that is spelled correctly.

speeker   speaker   speakr

NAME: _____ **DATE:** _____

SCORE

DIRECTIONS Read and answer each question.

1. (Y) (N)

1. Which word is always capitalized?

Name   Airline   New Mexico

2. (Y) (N)

2. Use an apostrophe to write *the propeller of the airplane* in another way.

3. (Y) (N)

_____

4. (Y) (N)

3. Add commas to the letter.

Dear Ricardo
You are the student of the month.
Congratulations! Your hard work has paid off.
Sincerely
Mr. Flores

5. (Y) (N)

6. (Y) (N)

___/6
Total

4. Write two adjectives about football.

_____   _____

5. Complete the sentence with two nouns.

I may see a crowd of _____
at a _____.

6. Circle the word that is spelled correctly.

Americka   Amarica   America

NAME: _____ DATE: _____

DIRECTIONS Read and answer each question.

1. Circle the words that need capital letters.

Do we travel north, south, east, or west to leave north dakota and arrive in south dakota?

2. Circle the correct contraction.

are'nt   dont'   wouldn't

3. Write two examples of contractions.

_____   _____

4. Circle the adverb in the sentence.

The team worked cooperatively to run the bake sale and earn money for their uniforms.

5. Complete the sentence with two nouns.

I may see a row of _____ in a _____.

6. Circle the word that is spelled correctly.

playd
plade
played

1. Ⓨ Ⓝ

2. Ⓨ Ⓝ

3. Ⓨ Ⓝ

4. Ⓨ Ⓝ

5. Ⓨ Ⓝ

6. Ⓨ Ⓝ

___ / 6
Total

NAME: _____ **DATE:** _____

1. Ⓨ Ⓝ

2. Ⓨ Ⓝ

3. Ⓨ Ⓝ

4. Ⓨ Ⓝ

5. Ⓨ Ⓝ

6. Ⓨ Ⓝ

___ / 6
Total

DIRECTIONS Read and answer each question.

1. Write a sentence about a place you like to visit.

_____

_____

2. Add punctuation to the letter greeting.

Dear Mr. Scott

3. Rewrite the sentence with a contraction.

Paul was not able to play at recess because of his cast.

_____

_____

4. Write an adjective to complete the sentence.

The man's _____ mustache made his face look interesting.

5. What is the past tense of *lose*?

losing   lost   loose

6. Circle the word that is spelled correctly.

draine   drayne   drain

NAME: _____ **DATE:** _____

DIRECTIONS   Read and answer each question.

1. Circle the word that needs a capital letter.

The store sold us a panasonic® television for our new house.

1. Ⓨ Ⓝ

2. Use an apostrophe to write *the car belonging to my dad* in another way.

_____

2. Ⓨ Ⓝ

3. Ⓨ Ⓝ

3. Write a sentence about the car using a contraction for *cannot*.

_____

_____

4. Ⓨ Ⓝ

4. Circle the adjectives in the sentence.

The tall skyscraper looked as if it gently touched the white clouds.

5. Ⓨ Ⓝ

6. Ⓨ Ⓝ

5. Circle the adverb in the sentence.

The plane flew loudly above our house.

___/ 6
Total

6. Circle the word that is spelled correctly.

hungry   hungrey   hungree

NAME: _____ **DATE:** _____

DIRECTIONS Read and answer each question.

1. (Y)(N)

2. (Y)(N)

3. (Y)(N)

4. (Y)(N)

5. (Y)(N)

6. (Y)(N)

___/6
Total

1. Write a sentence about your favorite month.

_____

_____

2. Add a contraction to complete the sentence.

Our family _____ decide on a restaurant.

3. Add commas to the letter.

Dear Bob
Thank you for coming to my party.
Your friend
Max

4. What would you call a group of people who have a similar interest?

a herd   a panel   a club

5. Circle the verb in the sentence.

Deb sat with her friends on the playground.

6. Circle the word that is spelled correctly.

wreck   reck   rek

NAME: _____ **DATE:** _____

DIRECTIONS Read and answer each question.

1. Which word should always be capitalized?

Pen   Mean   Europe

2. Write a possessive noun and an object it possesses.

_____

3. Add commas to the letter.

Dear manager
I'd like to apply for a job. I'm a responsible
worker.
Sincerely
Meredith

4. Write an adverb that could be used in the sentence.

Angela worked _____ to finish her
homework before dinner.

5. What is the past tense of *begin*?

begins   begun   began

6. Circle the word that is spelled correctly.

wealthy   wealthe   wealthie

1. Ⓨ Ⓝ

2. Ⓨ Ⓝ

3. Ⓨ Ⓝ

4. Ⓨ Ⓝ

5. Ⓨ Ⓝ

6. Ⓨ Ⓝ

___ / 6
Total

NAME: _____ DATE: _____

SCORE

1. Ⓨ Ⓝ

2. Ⓨ Ⓝ

3. Ⓨ Ⓝ

4. Ⓨ Ⓝ

5. Ⓨ Ⓝ

6. Ⓨ Ⓝ

___ / 6
Total

DIRECTIONS Read and answer each question.

1. Circle the words that need capital letters.

"Let's all travel to barbados for new year's day!" maria exclaimed.

2. Add a contraction that makes sense in this sentence.

The teacher _____ allow students to be in the room alone.

3. Write two contractions.

_____   _____

4. Circle the adverb to complete the sentence.

Quincy measured the table exactly with a ruler.

5. Write the past tense word in the blank

Who _____ us home from practice last week?
         (drive)

6. Write a word that includes the -less spelling pattern as in *fearless*.

_____

NAME: _____ DATE: _____

DIRECTIONS Read and answer each question.

1. Write the name of a nearby city or town.

_____

1. Ⓨ Ⓝ

2. Use an apostrophe to write *the house belonging to my neighbor* in another way.

_____

2. Ⓨ Ⓝ

3. Ⓨ Ⓝ

3. Write a sentence about a car. Include the contraction for *should not*.

_____

_____

4. Ⓨ Ⓝ

5. Ⓨ Ⓝ

4. Circle the adjectives in the sentence.

The brave skier definitely wanted to explore the mountain range.

6. Ⓨ Ⓝ

___ / 6
Total

5. Circle the adverb in the sentence.

The water flowed quickly out of the hose.

6. Write a word that includes the *pre-* spelling pattern as in *preview*.

_____

NAME: _____ **DATE:** _____

SCORE

DIRECTIONS Read and answer each question.

1. Ⓨ Ⓝ

2. Ⓨ Ⓝ

3. Ⓨ Ⓝ

4. Ⓨ Ⓝ

5. Ⓨ Ⓝ

6. Ⓨ Ⓝ

___ / 6
Total

1. Write the name of a nearby state.

_____

2. Write a sentence with a contraction.

_____

_____

3. Write two possessive nouns.

_____   _____

4. Many plural nouns end in -s or -es. Which noun does **not** follow this rule?

mouse   worm   plant

5. Circle the adverb in the sentence.

George endlessly worked on the yard until it was clean.

6. Write a word that includes the un- spelling pattern as in undone.

_____

NAME: _____ DATE: _____

DIRECTIONS Read and answer each question.

1. Why would you capitalize *Dawes Avenue* in a sentence?

_____

1. Ⓨ Ⓝ

2. Add a contraction to complete the sentence.

The baseball team _____ know the rules of the game.

2. Ⓨ Ⓝ

3. Ⓨ Ⓝ

3. Write an object that belongs to a family member using an apostrophe.

_____

4. Ⓨ Ⓝ

5. Ⓨ Ⓝ

4. Complete the sentence with a noun and a verb.

I belonged to a class of _____, and we

learned to _____.

6. Ⓨ Ⓝ

___ / 6
Total

5. Circle the pronoun in the sentence.

We were proud of ourselves for reaching the top of the mountain.

6. Write a word that includes the *re-* spelling pattern as in *rewrite*.

_____

NAME: _____ **DATE:** _____

DIRECTIONS Read and answer each question.

1. Which word is always capitalized?

Louisiana   Name   From

2. Use an apostrophe to write *the baseball that belongs to Michael* in another way.

_____

3. Add commas to the letter.

Dear second grader
I have loved teaching you. Have a great summer.
Sincerely
Your teacher

4. Write two adjectives about your favorite dessert.

_____   _____

5. Complete the sentence with a noun and a verb.

I can see a flock of _____ when
I _____.

6. Write a word that includes the *-er* spelling pattern as in *bigger*.

_____

NAME: _____ DATE: _____

DIRECTIONS Read and answer each question.

1. Circle the words that need capital letters.

"Is this train headed to davenport or rocklin?" the passenger asked the conductor.

1. Ⓨ Ⓝ

2. Ⓨ Ⓝ

2. Circle the correct contraction.

wa'snt   cann't   couldn't

3. Ⓨ Ⓝ

3. Circle the possessive noun in the sentence.

Jan's cat sadly ran away.

4. Ⓨ Ⓝ

4. Circle the adverb in the sentence.

The dancers moved gracefully during the routine.

5. Ⓨ Ⓝ

6. Ⓨ Ⓝ

5. Circle the noun in the sentence.

How is the weather?

___ / 6
Total

6. Write a word that includes the -*est* spelling pattern as in greatest.

_____

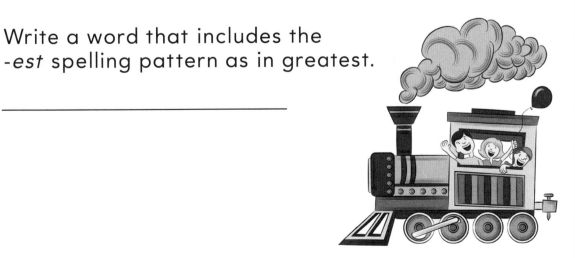

ANSWER KEY

Note: All sentences in the answer key include correct capitalization and punctuation. Also, words within sentences that students are to circle are indicated in bold.

Day 1
1. My family went to **Virginia**.
2. shouldn't
3. Dear John,
4. **The warm** cake was cooling on **the** rack.
5. The dog **sat** under the tree.
6. flight

Day 2
1. Christmas
2. won't
3. Love,
4. teeth
5. The car sped **quickly** to the train station.
6. taught

Day 3
1. The **San Francisco** map showed me where to go.
2. weren't
3. Dearest Lily,
4. child/children
5. The kids are not allowed to help **themselves** to dessert.
6. square

Day 4
1. Answers will vary.
2. a dog's bone
3. ,
4. Answers will vary.
5. men
6. brought

Day 5
1. Answers will vary.
2. a friend's party
3. Your friend,
4. The turtle moved **slowly** along the path.
5. sheep
6. fixture

Day 6
1. The King Deli has a special **menu** on Halloween.
2. Dear Nana,
3. Frank's cake
4. The **flock** of birds filled the sky.
5. I was not sure what to draw on the **blank** paper.
6. clown

Day 7
1. California
2. Love, Sydney
3. I'm
4. bouquet
5. I need to move my hand **carefully** while I paint.
6. slow

Day 8
1. Where can I find the **Main Street Library**?
2. Answers will vary.
3. aren't
4. **My** dad's **fancy** car goes fast down **the** street.
5. Let's play with a **deck** of cards.
6. needed

Day 9
1. Answers will vary.
2. my teacher's book
3. ,
4. Answers will vary.
5. Answers will vary.
6. each

Day 10
1. My favorite brand of granola bars is **Natural Bars**.
2. The artist's (or artists') work is very special to him.
3. Your student,
4. began
5. an army
6. both

Day 11
1. The islands in **Hawaii** are beautiful!
2. Answers will vary.
3. The bus driver **won't** pick up kids who are late.
4. **My** party took place on **a hot** day.
5. had
6. cow

Day 12
1. The store sells **Apple** computers.
2. can't
3. the tiger's cub
4. one car/two cars
5. My friend **gladly** said yes to the invitation.
6. coat

ANSWER KEY *(cont.)*

Day 13
1. Answers will vary.
2. You **can't** pick flowers from a person's garden!
3. Answers will vary.
4. a bouquet of flowers
5. The students can locate their book bags **themselves**.
6. watch

Day 14
1. Canada
2. Phoebe's hair
3. Dear Finn, Will you come to my house? My mom says that Monday is a good day. Your friend, Jesse
4. Answers will vary.
5. A large group of **men** toured the building.
6. fence

Day 15
1. Do you celebrate **Christmas** or a different holiday?
2. I don't want to go to Patrick's party.
3. won't, didn't, shouldn't
4. Jose's grandmother asked him to ride his bike **safely**.
5. Six **children** were in a group on the field trip.
6. flow

Day 16
1. Have you heard of the **Great Barrier Reef**?
2. Answers will vary.
3. I **can't** turn in my homework today.
4. **The blue** fish swam through **the clear** water.
5. The **people** boarded the bus in the morning.
6. mail, main

Day 17
1. The directions told me how to update my **Microsoft** software.
2. I've
3. Lily's coat
4. foot
5. The tiger **happily** ate its lunch in the sun.
6. sea, beach

Day 18
1. Answers will vary.
2. Soccer **wasn't** always my favorite sport.
3. Answers will vary.
4. an army of ants
5. Kiana is going to treat **herself** to a frozen yogurt after the big game.
6. toe

Day 19
1. Florida
2. my teacher's book
3. Dear Maya, I hope you have a great birthday. Your friend, Maria
4. Answers will vary.
5. Answers will vary.
6. neat

Day 20
1. holiday names
2. I shouldn't have to pick up Juan's clothes because that is his job!
3. can't, mustn't, we've
4. The field trip went **terribly** since we missed our bus.
5. Answers will vary.
6. blue

Day 21
1. Answers will vary.
2. Dear Mr. Franklin,
3. The police officer **should've** pulled over that car for speeding.
4. Answers will vary.
5. bought
6. change

Day 22
1. I like to use **Crayola** markers.
2. could've
3. Veronica's pair of shoes
4. Answers will vary.
5. **The strong** coffee was served in **a** mug.
6. since

Day 23
1. Answers will vary.
2. Why **can't** we take a ball out for recess?
3. Dear Editor, I think we need more parks. They are important for our health. Sincerely, Luis
4. chain of islands
5. Tasha is able to finish her homework **herself**.
6. dance

Day 24
1. Hawaii
2. the restaurant's pizza
3. Dear Mom, You are the best mom ever. Thank you for the new video game. Love, Joey
4. The car moved **slowly** through the parking lot.
5. shook
6. city

ANSWER KEY (cont.)

Day 25
1. brand names
2. My dad should've told me that Jack's mom was coming.
3. who'd, mustn't, isn't
4. Jessie arrived **promptly** as the school bell rang.
5. Yesterday was the day I **got** my braces.
6. age

Day 26
1. The capital of our country is **Washington**, D.C.
2. Dear Mom,
3. December **isn't** the best month for swimming in our pool.
4. **The frozen** dessert was **a** treat on **a hot** day.
5. The dentist looked at my **teeth** to check for cavities.
6. wheel

Day 27
1. Answers will vary.
2. we've
3. the school's mascot
4. sheep
5. The kitten **playfully** swatted the ball of yarn.
6. teacher

Day 28
1. Answers will vary.
2. Kids **shouldn't** spend too much time playing video games.
3. I'm, can't, could've
4. a class of students
5. Our teacher told us to not grade **ourselves** on the quiz.
6. stretch

Day 29
1. Arkansas
2. the bakery's cookie
3. Dear Owner, I was in your store today. Your employee was very helpful. We are so glad your store is near our house. Sincerely, A happy customer
4. Answers will vary.
5. Answers will vary.
6. shook

Day 30
1. Should we go to **New Orleans** or **Fort Lauderdale** on our vacation?
2. The postal worker cannot deliver mail to our house because of Shannon's dog.
3. didn't, could've, mightn't
4. The girls moved **quickly** to catch the ice cream truck.
5. Answers will vary.
6. laid

Day 31
1. Answers will vary.
2. Dear Principal Smith, Would you consider having the cafeteria serve dessert on Fridays? Please think about it. Sincerely, Jaden
3. wasn't
4. **The green** grass grew quickly under **the warm** sun.
5. The **fish** were colorful in the ocean.
6. Answers will vary.

Day 32
1. Some of my favorite movies are made by **Pixar**.
2. they'll
3. Mario's lunch
4. a school
5. The squirrel **mischievously** ate the nuts from the tree in our garden.
6. Answers will vary.

Day 33
1. We really like to go to **Newport** to stay at the beach.
2. We **didn't** see the lions at the zoo because they were napping.
3. Veronica's homework was missing from her backpack.
4. a forest
5. Mom said, "I want you to take care of your chores **yourself**."
6. soak

Day 34
1. Easter
2. Yummy Pie's pizza
3. Dear Grandma, When are you coming for a visit? I miss you very much. Love, Sofia
4. Answers will vary.
5. Answers will vary.
6. soap

Day 35
1. days of the week
2. Keegan can't believe that Jason's sister could be that mean.
3. aren't, should've, didn't
4. The airplane landed **safely** after a rough ride.
5. Answers will vary.
6. about

Day 36
1. Pollution is harming the **Atlantic Ocean.**
2. I **don't** know where **I'm** going to eat lunch today.
3. the coat's buttons
4. I noticed **the speeding** car race down **the** street.
5. The **mice** scurried into the hole in the ground.
6. Answers will vary.

ANSWER KEY *(cont.)*

Day 37
1. I would like to visit **Paris**, France.
2. I'm
3. **Mario's** pool felt very refreshing on a hot day.
4. man
5. Scientists **rarely** see endangered species.
6. Answers will vary.

Day 38
1. Answers will vary.
2. Vanilla **isn't** my favorite choice for ice cream.
3. Dear Frank**,** Can you come over for a sleepover tonight? Your friend**,** Marco
4. a swarm of bees
5. What will **you** do with **yourself** over vacation?
6. poem

Day 39
1. Montana
2. the ant's antenna
3. Dear Nancy**,**
4. Answers will vary.
5. Answers will vary.
6. grew

Day 40
1. months of the year
2. Drivers don't always know that the car**'s** gas is almost out.
3. doesn't, won't, haven't
4. My bus driver greets me **cheerfully** every morning.
5. I had to excuse **myself** from the table.
6. Answers will vary.

Day 41
1. Our vacation to **London, England**, was the best part of the summer.
2. Answers will vary.
3. The students **should've** studied harder for the challenging test.
4. **The healthy** plant continued to grow **many** leaves.
5. The **hostesses** cut the **cakes** at **parties**.
6. grain

Day 42
1. Where can I find **Park View School**?
2. won't
3. the flower's petal
4. child
5. The zookeeper talked **excitedly** about the new lions.
6. goes

Day 43
1. Labor Day, North Pole
2. **Chloe's** backyard has the best swing set!
3. Dear Mr. Evans**,** Our classroom really needs a new computer. Sincerely**,** The students in room 5
4. a litter
5. The elephant tried to cool **itself** with water.
6. please

Day 44
1. The view from the top of **Mount Everest** was the most beautiful thing I have ever seen.
2. Shelly's dog
3. Dear Felix**,**
4. Answers will vary.
5. Answers will vary.
6. rock

Day 45
1. The train will stop at the towns of **Jackson**, **Hollywood**, and **Parker**.
2. Maria couldn't see that her sister's toy was under the bed.
3. shouldn't, they're, aren't
4. Jose's mom divided the cookie **evenly**.
5. Answers will vary.
6. Answers will vary.

Day 46
1. Henry wants to go to the **Amazon Rainforest** for **New Year's Day**.
2. Answers will vary.
3. **They're** the best friends I could ever want.
4. **The warm** muffin was on **the** menu at our **special** restaurant.
5. Answers will vary.
6. took

Day 47
1. It's a product brand.
2. who's
3. the cat's food
4. mouse
5. Kara **lovingly** hugged her brother before he **quickly** walked to the bus stop.
6. wool

Day 48
1. Answers will vary.
2. My sister got into trouble, and now **I'm** very sad.
3. Answers will vary.
4. a herd
5. Lily jumped in the puddle because she could not help **herself**.
6. took

ANSWER KEY *(cont.)*

Day 49
1. Answers will vary.
2. Pablo's phone
3. Dear Mom, Thank you for the birthday party. Love, Luke
4. Answers will vary.
5. Answers will vary.
6. such

Day 50
1. Jack's favorite baseball team is from **San Francisco**.
2. The teacher didn't want to give directions until the student's (or students') talking had stopped.
3. I'll, couldn't, she'll
4. Good friends almost always play **happily** together.
5. Answers will vary.
6. hour

Day 51
1. Check the weather in **Springfield** and **Salem**.
2. Answers will vary.
3. **I'd** like to sing, but I **can't** sing in class.
4. **The happy** baby wanted to crawl to **the exciting** toy.
5. I **kept** a diary of what I **did** each day.
6. Answers will vary.

Day 52
1. The video game can work on **Microsoft** or **Apple** machines.
2. how'd
3. the chair's leg
4. I **saw** the customer pay for the groceries.
5. The rain fell **quietly** while I slept **peacefully** in my bed.
6. Answers will vary.

Day 53
1. Answers will vary.
2. Rap music **shouldn't** be played at school.
3. Answers will vary.
4. a chest of drawers
5. The door was unlocked, so we let **ourselves** in the house.
6. Answers will vary.

Day 54
1. Answers will vary.
2. piano's keys
3. Dear neighbor, I accidentally hit the ball through your window. I can help fix it. Your neighbor, Henry
4. Answers will vary.
5. Answers will vary.
6. tail

Day 55
1. Answers will vary.
2. Answers will vary.
3. Answers will vary.
4. Answers will vary.
5. Answers will vary.
6. meet

Day 56
1. The airplane flew from **Las Vegas** to **New York**.
2. Dear Coach, I learned a lot about soccer from you. Your player, Romeo
3. they'll
4. Naomi slept with **her fluffy** bear on **a stormy** night.
5. Basketball **halves** are 12 minutes each.
6. Answers will vary.

Day 57
1. My mom buys the healthy cereal made by **Nature's Best**.
2. who'll
3. Mariela's coat
4. a mountain range
5. The bicycle went by **quickly** as it went down the hill.
6. Answers will vary.

Day 58
1. The **Red Sea** is amazing to see.
2. **He's** my best friend, so I chose him to be on my team.
3. Jack's baseball team made the playoffs.
4. team
5. Violet said, "Can you please take care of our puppy **yourself**?"
6. Answers will vary.

Day 59
1. Thanksgiving
2. the lion's prey
3. Dear Dad, I am very sorry that I lost your keys. I will help you find them. Your son, Pablo
4. Answers will vary.
5. Answers will vary.
6. Answers will vary.

Day 60
1. proper nouns
2. Luke's birthday guest list includes Leo and Leo's sister.
3. where's, how'd, you've
4. Answers will vary.
5. A group of **men** worked together to push the car.
6. boot

ANSWER KEY *(cont.)*

Day 61
1. Answers will vary.
2. a friend's pet
3. I'm
4. Answers will vary.
5. **Cities** are great places to visit.
6. Answers will vary.

Day 62
1. The book was just published by **Teacher Created Materials**.
2. mom's hair
3. Ted's ice cream
4. Answers will vary.
5. The door creaked **slowly** as I opened it.
6. Answers will vary.

Day 63
1. The police went to **North Hanford** on a call.
2. **Why's** Ana not in school today?
3. Aiden's turn on the computer is today.
4. a crew
5. "I will just do it **myself**," Sara said.
6. Answers will vary.

Day 64
1. Colorado
2. Oscar's toy car
3. Dear George, Will you bring your trucks to our play date? Your friend, Jeffrey
4. The student **sat** at a new desk yesterday.
5. Answers will vary.
6. cave

Day 65
1. cities
2. Dad couldn't go to Sarah's game today.
3. mustn't, hadn't, aren't
4. Jesse **hid** under the bed to trick his mom.
5. The **children** loved the summer camp.
6. kick

Day 66
1. Have you ever been to **West Virginia**?
2. Answers will vary.
3. Answers will vary.
4. **The yellow** flower poked out of **the wet** soil.
5. The **women** read books to relax.
6. Answers will vary.

Day 67
1. My favorite gift was blocks made by **Lego**.
2. could've
3. Fred's candy
4. a team
5. We have to leave **soon** to get a table.
6. Answers will vary.

Day 68
1. There are many deserts in **Arizona**.
2. **They'll** meet us at the concert.
3. Jackson's skateboard was brand new.
4. Answers will vary.
5. Grace said, "You cannot vote for **yourself** in this game."
6. lodge

Day 69
1. America, Africa
2. Chloe's water
3. Dear Mom, Happy Mother's Day! You are the best. Love, Nina
4. Answers will vary.
5. Answers will vary.
6. soil

Day 70
1. countries
2. Harper's dog shouldn't be off the leash.
3. I've, we're, mustn't
4. She is **nearly** six years old because her birthday is next week.
5. The **men** played football all morning.
6. sleep

Day 71
1. Is anyone able to visit the **South Pole**?
2. the restaurant's owner
3. mustn't
4. **The blue** bird sat on **a small** branch.
5. My dentist wants me to take care of my **teeth**.
6. when

Day 72
1. I really love toys made by the **Lego** company.
2. I'll
3. the lion's food
4. a pack
5. Stephanie **shyly** asked to borrow the jacket.
6. such

ANSWER KEY (cont.)

Day 73
1. The beaches in **Florida** are quite pretty.
2. We **wouldn't** leave you alone!
3. Jacob's football had no air.
4. a pack
5. Dad shouted, "Take good care of **yourself**, Iris!"
6. loyal

Day 74
1. Chicago
2. Brady's ticket
3. Dear Luis**,** Will you come to my party? It is on Saturday. Your friend**,** Sam
4. Answers will vary.
5. Parker **told** a secret to his sister.
6. much

Day 75
1. city names
2. Don't you want to go to Milo's party?
3. I've, mustn't, they'll
4. I **partially** opened the window to let in cool air.
5. Our class **sat** for our school picture.
6. late

Day 76
1. The boat sailed on the **Indian Ocean**.
2. The cat **doesn't** see that **she's** sitting on a toy.
3. the house's roof
4. **The happy** man smiled at **his young** child.
5. Sam's **feet** were hurting.
6. Answers will vary.

Day 77
1. My favorite show is on **Cartoon Network**.
2. they're
3. The **dog's** leash was too tight.
4. goose
5. Mom **calmly** told me to come inside.
6. Answers will vary.

Day 78
1. There are many old buildings in **Rome, Italy**.
2. mustn't
3. Answers will vary.
4. a herd
5. Jade hurt **herself** when **she** fell.
6. height

Day 79
1. Iowa
2. the rock's edge
3. Dear Sasha,
4. **The lifelong** friends watched **the intense** game.
5. We cheered **loudly** to support our team.
6. three

Day 80
1. names of cities
2. Harry isn't afraid of Peter's dog.
3. couldn't, they'll, where's
4. The lock fit **tightly** on the door.
5. I should clean **myself** up before I go to sleep.
6. Answers will vary.

Day 81
1. Where is the **Nile River**?
2. I **mustn't** get a bad report from my teacher.
3. the pot's lid
4. **The shiny** penny stuck out of **the sandy** beach.
5. The **women** boarded the bus at the stop.
6. Answers will vary.

Day 82
1. I love to watch cartoons on **Nickelodeon**.
2. she's
3. **Nola's dog** ran on the beach.
4. mouse
5. The dolphin dove **deeply** in the water.
6. Answers will vary.

Day 83
1. Answers will vary.
2. **Who'd** like to have dessert tonight?
3. Answers will vary.
4. Answers will vary.
5. Answers will vary.
6. Answers will vary.

Day 84
1. The boat ride on **Lake Erie** was very peaceful.
2. Hank's apple
3. Dear Sid,
4. Answers will vary.
5. Answers will vary.
6. Answers will vary.

ANSWER KEY *(cont.)*

Day 85
1. Answers will vary.
2. A giraffe's neck can't fit in a short building.
3. I'm, you've, you'll
4. Who **sat** at the table this morning?
5. The **women** ate lunch and then went back to work.
6. tough

Day 86
1. The sun sets over the **Pacific Ocean**.
2. I don't know where I'll go after school.
3. Jack's bike
4. Diego wants **warm** soup for **his birthday** dinner.
5. The **teeth are** very loose.
6. Answers will vary.

Day 87
1. Our computer lab has **Microsoft** software.
2. couldn't
3. **Rita's doll** is very cute.
4. men, women
5. Nora weighs **exactly** 70 pounds.
6. Answers will vary.

Day 88
1. The police officer from **Hartford** was on patrol.
2. Some insects **aren't** cute and cuddly.
3. Answers will vary.
4. Answers will vary.
5. "Take care of **yourself** and feel better," Maria told Ana.
6. most

Day 89
1. Can I have **Quaker** oatmeal for breakfast?
2. the leopard's spots
3. Dear Ava,
4. Answers will vary.
5. Answers will vary.
6. ocean

Day 90
1. Where is **Wisconsin** on the map?
2. She's always safe on her sister's bike.
3. couldn't, must've, isn't
4. My mom greets me **happily** each day.
5. The **children** in class all sat still.
6. Answers will vary.

Day 91
1. The **Mississippi River** flows for many miles.
2. I **can't** eat the cookie because **I'm** full.
3. Olivia's sweater
4. **The surprise** party was **a fun** event.
5. The **geese** lived on the farm.
6. Answers will vary.

Day 92
1. I want to order a book from the **Scholastic** book order.
2. who's
3. **Sophia's bike** is not working.
4. deer
5. I walk my dog **daily**.
6. true

Day 93
1. Answers will vary.
2. Answers will vary.
3. Answers will vary.
4. **The young** child danced to **the loud** music.
5. The boy **excitedly** greeted his neighbor.
6. tight

Day 94
1. Answers will vary.
2. **How'll** you get home from school?
3. Sincerely,
4. Answers will vary.
5. Answers will vary.
6. hero

Day 95
1. names of countries
2. The ship's captain can't stop working while sailing.
3. can't, I've, she's
4. **The long** worm slithered through **the warm** ground.
5. The caterpillar moves **slowly** on the leaf.
6. Answers will vary.

Day 96
1. Can you canoe on **Lake Michigan**?
2. **Won't** you come with me to **Jan's** party?
3. Erik's piano
4. I ate **the delicious blueberry** muffin.
5. I **quickly** ate my breakfast.
6. Answers will vary.

ANSWER KEY (cont.)

Day 97

1. Does this store sell **Levi** jeans?
2. you'll
3. **Jose's** water bottle was orange.
4. ox
5. Marco **quietly** slipped out of his bed.
6. Answers will vary.

Day 98

1. Answers will vary.
2. **Where'd** you like to go after school?
3. Dear Pam**,** I saw you had a cast. I just wanted to check in with you. How did you hurt your arm? Your friend**,** Michael
4. a pack of dogs
5. How did you hurt **yourself**?
6. change

Day 99

1. Texas
2. the table's leg
3. Dear Mr. Jackson,
4. Answers will vary.
5. Answers will vary.
6. air

Day 100

1. proper nouns
2. The workers aren't happy about work, so they're going on strike.
3. we'll, he's, you're
4. The leaf fell **softly** from the tree.
5. The kids hid **themselves** in the forest.
6. Answers will vary.

Day 101

1. Violet lives on **David Drive**.
2. **She's** mad that **he'd** been so mean to her.
3. the backpack's zipper
4. **The small**, **blue** bird chirped happily.
5. Lily's **teeth** were wiggly.
6. Answers will vary.

Day 102

1. The art teacher passed out the **Crayola** colored pencils.
2. could've
3. **Kai's notebook** was missing.
4. foot
5. Nina **usually** walks to school with Fran.
6. Answers will vary.

Day 103

1. My mom buys **Horizon** milk for our family.
2. Tomatoes **aren't** vegetables. They are fruits.
3. Dear Mom**,** I want a new book. Will you take me to the store? Love**,** Luis
4. Answers will vary.
5. Ava packed **her** suitcase for the sleepover.
6. paid

Day 104

1. Oregon, Mexico, Twin Lake
2. the bike's pedal
3. Dear Will,
4. Answers will vary.
5. Answers will vary.
6. place

Day 105

1. I always choose the **Kellogg's** cereal to eat.
2. They'll be there when she's ready for them.
3. I'm, they'll, must've
4. The spider moved **quickly** to get to the web.
5. I can't hear **myself** think when it is this loud!
6. Answers will vary.

Day 106

1. **New Hampshire** is where my grandparents live.
2. **She's** my best friend because **she's** kind and funny.
3. Martha's ring
4. **The big yellow** school bus takes students to school.
5. The woman drove **safely** with an infant in the back seat.
6. Answers will vary.

Day 107

1. Our gym clothes at school are made by **Hanes**.
2. when'd
3. **My neighbor's trampoline** was a lot of fun!
4. moose
5. Some teachers **rarely** sit all day long.
6. Answers will vary.

Day 108

1. Answers will vary.
2. **When's** the best time to do your homework?
3. Dear Dad**,** I really need your help with my bike. I can't fix it. Your son**,** Hector
4. a pair of shoes
5. I can make breakfast for **myself**.
6. very

ANSWER KEY *(cont.)*

Day 109
1. **Yesterday**, **Mrs.** **Dawes** gave us too much homework.
2. the computer's keyboard
3. Dear Shannon,
4. Answers will vary.
5. Answers will vary.
6. life

Day 110
1. **Do** you want to play tennis tonight, **Jesse**?
2. The baby's bottle is empty, so she's crying.
3. where'd   she's   they'll
4. The python slithered **silently** across the ground.
5. "Students, clean up after **yourselves**," said the teacher.
6. Answers will vary.

Day 111
1. On **Halloween**, we will be traveling to **Connecticut**.
2. Answers will vary.
3. Dogs **aren't** always friendly animals.
4. I like to sit in **the comfortable black** chair in **the living** room.
5. Answers will vary.
6. clump

Day 112
1. It is the name of a state.
2. she's
3. the mouse's tail
4. deer
5. The sun shone **brightly** as I played **happily** at the park.
6. move

Day 113
1. It is the name of a holiday.
2. At my neighbor's house, **they've** got six chickens.
3. Answers will vary.
4. a litter
5. "Keep your hands to **yourself**," scolded Mom.
6. Answers will vary.

Day 114
1. Answers will vary.
2. Kira's ears
3. Dear Jeff**,** You are a great kid. I just need you to clean your room! Love**,** Mom
4. Answers will vary.
5. Answers will vary.
6. great

Day 115
1. **Ned's** favorite football team is from **Pittsburgh**.
2. This soup isn't my favorite, but it's actually pretty good!
3. I'm, didn't, we'll
4. rode
5. Answers will vary.
6. tower

Day 116
1. Today, we head to **Columbia** and **Durham**.
2. Answers will vary.
3. **I'd** like to eat, but I **can't** yet.
4. **The rude** man cut in line, and **the angry** customers complained.
5. We **swam** in the pool for fun.
6. Answers will vary.

Day 117
1. I prefer to buy the **Mead** brand of folders for my school work.
2. how'll
3. the hospital's bed
4. I **taught** my friend how to play soccer.
5. The music played **loudly** while I lay **quietly** in my bed.
6. Answers will vary.

Day 118
1. Do you celebrate **Easter** with your grandparents?
2. Third graders **can't** be helpers in the cafeteria.
3. Answers will vary.
4. rows
5. The runners surprised **themselves** with their speed.
6. Answers will vary.

Day 119
1. Answers will vary.
2. my dog's hair
3. Dear Steven**,** Your reading has improved this year! I am very proud of you. Your teacher**,** Mrs. Hanson
4. Answers will vary.
5. Answers will vary.
6. rail

Day 120
1. Answers will vary.
2. Answers will vary.
3. Answers will vary.
4. Answers will vary.
5. Answers will vary.
6. greet

ANSWER KEY *(cont.)*

Day 121
1. Mariela had to prepare for a **Valentine's Day** party.
2. Answers will vary.
3. Answers will vary.
4. **The fluffy** pillow felt **comfortable** against **my** head.
5. Answers will vary.
6. book

Day 122
1. It is the name of a product's brand.
2. hadn't
3. Maria's hairband
4. foot
5. Tina **loudly** screamed at her mom, who was **blindly** crossing in front of a car.
6. cool

Day 123
1. Mom will decide how long we can play with our **Nintendo** game.
2. **That's** not how I like my friends to treat me.
3. Answers will vary.
4. a panel
5. "What will I do with **myself** today?" Ana wondered.
6. took

Day 124
1. The time between **Thanksgiving** and **Christmas** goes by very quickly.
2. Russ's sister
3. Dear Mom**,** Thank you for being a wonderful mom. Love**,** Amanda
4. Answers will vary.
5. Answers will vary.
6. touch

Day 125
1. Are you rooting for the team from **Texas** or **Arkansas**?
2. She won't take medicine unless it's mixed with something.
3. I'm, can't, she'd
4. The sisters swam **happily** together.
5. Answers will vary.
6. our

Day 126
1. The bus will stop in **Brighton**, **Newberg**, and **Warren**.
2. Answers will vary.
3. **I'd** like to go home, but **I'll** stay longer.
4. **The small** bird flapped **its blue** wings and flew away.
5. I **tore** the paper for my art project.
6. Answers will vary.

Day 127
1. Can we go to the **Apple** store and buy a new part for our computer?
2. might've
3. the dog's fur
4. I **woke** in the morning when the sun **came** up.
5. The phone rang **loudly**, so I jumped up **suddenly**.
6. Answers will vary.

Day 128
1. How do you celebrate **Martin Luther King Jr.'s** birthday?
2. Bullying **isn't** tolerated at school.
3. Answers will vary.
4. Answers will vary.
5. My friend and I were hungry, so we helped **ourselves** to a snack.
6. Answers will vary.

Day 129
1. **Our** family is going out of town in **August**.
2. a horse's mane
3. Dear Hank**,** I am sorry I hurt your feelings. Please forgive me. Your neighbor**,** Joe
4. Answers will vary.
5. Answers will vary.
6. hail

Day 130
1. Answers will vary.
2. Answers will vary.
3. Answers will vary.
4. Answers will vary.
5. Answers will vary.
6. seat

Day 131
1. **I** can't believe it is almost spring break.
2. My brother**'s** friend has a great game called *Baseball Fan*.
3. that is, cannot
4. Answers will vary.
5. wrote
6. range

Day 132
1. The art teacher shows the students how to use the **Elmer's** glue carefully.
2. would've
3. Answers may vary, but should include *friend's game*
4. Answers will vary.
5. Wes has **red** hair, and it makes him look **unique**.
6. rinse

ANSWER KEY (cont.)

Day 133
1. Answers will vary.
2. Why **won't** the group start getting its work done?
3. Dear dentist**,** I am nervous to see you. I have not been flossing like you told me to. Your patient**,** Ella
4. a bunch of bananas
5. After a lot of practice, Claire could swim in the deep end by **herself**.
6. balance

Day 134
1. Utah
2. your friend's mother
3. Dear Dad**,** I am sorry you broke your leg. May I sign your cast? Your daughter**,** Alice
4. Answers will vary.
5. made
6. pity

Day 135
1. continent names
2. Gus wasn't sure that the pool's heater was turned on because the water was cold.
3. what's, mightn't, I've
4. Sophie ran out on the soccer field **quickly** so that she had time to practice.
5. The boss **paid** his workers once a month.
6. page

Day 136
1. The states of **North Carolina** and **South Carolina** border each other.
2. Dear Mom**,**
3. Air pollution **isn't** always visible, but **it's** still all around us.
4. **The brown** bear walked along **the icy** river, looking for **fresh** salmon to eat.
5. I don't know if the **women** work at the library.
6. heal

Day 137
1. It is a holiday.
2. why'd
3. our school's garden
4. wool
5. Who can ride a scooter **quickly** without getting hurt?
6. preacher

Day 138
1. Answers will vary.
2. The teacher **should've** warned us that we were having a test so we could have studied.
3. I'll, couldn't, here's
4. a faculty of teachers
5. You are not allowed to have **yourself** as a secret buddy.
6. stitch

Day 139
1. I wanted to wake up early and make breakfast for my mom the morning of **Mother's Day**.
2. My friend**'s** so nice. I am lucky to know her.
3. we would (or we had), let us
4. Answers will vary.
5. Answers will vary.
6. took

Day 140
1. **Central America** is directly north of **South America**.
2. The dog park isn't open because the park's gates are broken and dogs might escape.
3. couldn't, might've
4. Answers will vary.
5. Answers will vary.
6. wade

Day 141
1. Answers will vary.
2. Dear Mom and Dad**,**
3. The rain **won't** stop, so let's go inside.
4. Answers will vary.
5. caught
6. range

Day 142
1. **Whenever** I have a cold, I sleep with a **Kleenex** box next to my bed.
2. how is, how has
3. Answers will vary.
4. The police car sped **quickly** down the road.
5. **The tall** woman has **beautiful, long** hair.
6. cough

Day 143
1. Answers will vary.
2. The artwork **can't** fit on the wall because **it's** too big.
3. Answers will vary.
4. The baby piglet had **found** his mother and cuddled with her.
5. The ant can carry huge, heavy objects by **itself**.
6. happiness

Day 144
1. Vermont
2. Sheila's pencil
3. Answers will vary.
4. Answers will vary.
5. paid
6. confusion

ANSWER KEY (cont.)

Day 145
1. Answers will vary.
2. The seal should've watched out more carefully for those killer whales.
3. who'll, there's
4. The students **busily** put away their backpacks to start their day.
5. Yesterday I **meant** to get my bag, but I forgot it.
6. addition

Day 146
1. Should we go to **Hawaii** for summer vacation?
2. why is, why has
3. Answers will vary.
4. **The prickly** cactus bloomed and is covered with **red** flowers.
5. Would the **men** be able to check the engine on my car?
6. thoughtful

Day 147
1. Did you know that the capital of **Italy** is **Rome** or that the capital of **Germany** is **Berlin**?
2. Answers will vary.
3. the bull's horns
4. sheep
5. The kitten **playfully** swatted the ball of yarn.
6. brightness

Day 148
1. Answers will vary.
2. I hope that **you've** learned an important lesson about being a good friend.
3. we've, she'll, who'd
4. an audience
5. Answers will vary.
6. direction

Day 149
1. New Year's Day
2. the house's icicle
3. Answers will vary.
4. Answers will vary.
5. Answers will vary.
6. brightest

Day 150
1. Some people decided to travel to **Omaha**, while others headed the other way, to **Topeka**.
2. Kevin's aunt isn't the nicest person in the world.
3. don't, won't
4. We visited Grandpa in the hospital and **cheerfully** told him to feel better.
5. Answers will vary.
6. select

Day 151
1. Answers will vary.
2. they would, they had
3. The librarian **must've** set the book aside for me because I **don't** see it here.
4. a panel
5. wrote
6. exchange

Day 152
1. Our family loves to watch fireworks on the **Fourth** of **July**.
2. aren't, it's, wasn't
3. what is, is not
4. Answers will vary.
5. **The new** computer was quite **a nice** surprise.
6. determine

Day 153
1. Answers will vary.
2. The principal **wouldn't** tell us which class won the pizza party until the end of the day.
3. Dear Mason, You are working hard. Keep it up! Sincerely, Principal Jefferson
4. a band
5. Answers will vary.
6. represent

Day 154
1. Washington, Halloween
2. Noah's robot
3. the scientist's time machine
4. a set
5. stung
6. geometric

Day 155
1. **Jayden's** family was very excited. They were together for a party.
2. "A new video game! It's exactly what I wanted," yelled Scott.
3. could not, it is
4. Olivia cleaned her dirty room **promptly** before her friends saw it.
5. Olivia cleaned **her dirty** room promptly before **her close** friends saw it.
6. grateful

Day 156
1. The capital of **China** is **Beijing**.
2. Dear Aiden,
3. The storm caused us to lose power, so we **couldn't** watch television.
4. **The slimy** monster had **eight** heads and **red** eyes.
5. I saw **mice** in the basement.
6. sphere

ANSWER KEY *(cont.)*

Day 157
1. I'd love to travel to **Asia** to see **Japan**, **China**, **Thailand**, and the **Philippines**.
2. can't, we've, shouldn't
3. the princess's tiara
4. bison
5. The puppy **playfully** nipped at the chew toy.
6. happiness

Day 158
1. Answers will vary.
2. We go to my grandparents' house a lot, and **they're** always happy to see us.
3. where'd, how's, who's
4. Answers will vary.
5. **Our** class cannot wait to show **ourselves** off in **our** costumes for the play.
6. second Day

159
1. ice cream flavors
2. Fiona's scarf
3. Answers will vary.
4. Answers will vary.
5. Answers will vary.
6. dreamer

Day 160
1. Would you like to see pictures from our trip to **Indonesia** and **Vietnam**?
2. The neighbor's house is very scary, so we can't go in it alone.
3. shouldn't, would've
4. Answers will vary.
5. Answers will vary.
6. reason

Day 161
1. Answers will vary.
2. Dear Professor Stevens,
3. The baby **didn't** like to be in the crib alone.
4. Answers will vary.
5. found
6. change

Day 162
1. The store sold a lot of school supplies, including **Crayola** markers and **Bic** ballpoint pens.
2. would have, could have
3. Christina's new jeans
4. Answers will vary.
5. **The bright** light kept us up through **the long** night.
6. direction

Day 163
1. It is a name of a person.
2. Answers will vary, but should include the contraction *can't*.
3. have not, were not
4. Answers will vary.
5. My younger sister is still learning how to walk all by **herself**.
6. revise

Day 164
1. location
2. the fire's spark
3. Answers will vary, but should include the contraction *should've*.
4. Answers will vary.
5. got
6. Answers will vary.

Day 165
1. Answers will vary.
2. Answers will vary.
3. Answers will vary.
4. The clock ticked **continually** throughout the day.
5. I **heard** the playground rules have changed.
6. Answers will vary.

Day 166
1. The country of **Haiti** is part of an island in the **Caribbean**.
2. Answers will vary, but should include the contraction *might've*.
3. have not, had not
4. Answers will vary.
5. Answers will vary.
6. Answers will vary.

Day 167
1. Memorial Day, Thanksgiving
2. I'm, she's
3. Lucas's toothbrush
4. Answers will vary.
5. Answers will vary.
6. Answers will vary.

Day 168
1. Answers will vary.
2. The cafeteria **must've** served something special.
3. I'll, couldn't, would've
4. a herd of cows
5. We must protect **ourselves** by always wearing bike helmets while riding.
6. speaker

ANSWER KEY (cont.)

Day 169
1. New Mexico
2. the airplane's propeller
3. Dear Ricardo, You are the student of the month. Congratulations! Your hard work has paid off. Sincerely, Mr. Flores
4. Answers will vary.
5. Answers will vary.
6. America

Day 170
1. Do we travel north, south, east, or west to leave **North Dakota** and arrive in **South Dakota**?
2. wouldn't
3. Answers will vary.
4. The team worked **cooperatively** to run the bake sale and earn money for their uniforms.
5. Answers will vary.
6. played

Day 171
1. Answers will vary.
2. Dear Mr. Scott**,**
3. Paul **wasn't** able to play at recess because of his cast.
4. Answers will vary.
5. lost
6. drain

Day 172
1. The store sold us a **Panasonic** television for our new house.
2. my dad's car
3. Answers will vary, but should include the contraction *can't*.
4. **The tall** skyscraper looked as if it gently touched **the white** clouds.
5. The plane flew **loudly** above our house.
6. hungry

Day 173
1. Answers will vary.
2. Possible answers: can't, won't, didn't, shouldn't
3. Dear Bob, Thank you for coming to my party. Your friend, Max
4. a club
5. Deb **sat** with her friends on the playground.
6. wreck

Day 174
1. Europe
2. Answers will vary.
3. Dear manager, I'd like to apply for a job. I'm a responsible worker. Sincerely, Meredith
4. Answers will vary.
5. began
6. wealthy

Day 175
1. "Let's all travel to **Barbados** for **New Year's Day**!" **Maria** exclaimed.
2. Possible answers: can't, won't, didn't, shouldn't, wouldn't, couldn't, doesn't
3. Answers will vary.
4. Quincy measured the table **exactly** with a ruler.
5. Who **drove** us home from practice last week?
6. Answers will vary.

Day 176
1. Answers will vary.
2. my neighbor's house
3. Answers will vary, but should include the contraction *shouldn't*.
4. **The brave** skier definitely wanted to explore **the mountain** range.
5. The water flowed **quickly** out of the hose.
6. Answers will vary.

Day 177
1. Answers will vary.
2. Answers will vary.
3. Answers will vary.
4. mouse
5. George **endlessly** worked on the yard until it was clean.
6. Answers will vary.

Day 178
1. It is a street name.
2. Possible answers: didn't, won't, doesn't, wouldn't
3. Answers will vary.
4. Answers will vary.
5. We were proud of **ourselves** for reaching the top of the mountain.
6. Answers will vary.

Day 179
1. Louisiana
2. Michael's baseball
3. Dear second grader, I have loved teaching you. Have a great summer. Sincerely, Your teacher
4. Answers will vary.
5. Answers will vary.
6. Answers will vary.

Day 180
1. "Is this train headed to **Davenport** or **Rocklin**?" the passenger asked the conductor.
2. couldn't
3. **Jan's** cat sadly ran away.
4. The dancers moved **gracefully** during the routine.
5. How is the **weather**?
6. Answers will vary.

REFERENCES CITED

Haussamen, Brock. 2014. "Some Questions and Answers About Grammar." Retrieved from http://www.ateg.org/grammar/qna.php.

Hillocks, George, Jr., and Michael W. Smith. 1991. "Grammar and Usage." In *Handbook of Research on Teaching the English Language Arts.* James Flood, Julie M. Jensen, Diane Lapp, and James R. Squire. New York: Macmillan.

Hodges, Richard E. 1991. "The Conventions of Writing." In *Handbook of Research on Teaching the English Language Arts.* James Flood, Julie M. Jensen, Diane Lapp, and James R. Squire. New York: Macmillan.

———. 2003. "Grammar and Literacy Learning." In *Handbook of Research on Teaching the English Language Arts*, 2nd ed. James Flood, Julie M. Jensen, Diane Lapp, and James R. Squire. New York: Macmillan.

Lederer, Richard. 1987. *Anguished English: An Anthology of Accidental Assaults upon Our Language.* New York: Dell.

Marzano, Robert J. 2010. When Practice Makes Perfect. . .Sense. *Educational Leadership* 68(3): 81–83.

Truss, Lynne. 2003. *Eats, Shoots and Leaves: The Zero Tolerance Approach to Punctuation.* New York: Gotham Books.

DIGITAL RESOURCES

Accessing the Digital Resources

The digital resources can be downloaded by following these steps:

1. Go to **www.tcmpub.com/digital**

2. Sign in or create an account.

3. Click **Redeem Content** and enter the ISBN number, located on page 2 and the back cover, into the appropriate field on the website.

4. Respond to the prompts using the book to view your account and available digital content.

5. Choose the digital resources you would like to download. You can download all the files at once, or you can download a specific group of files.

ISBN:
9781425811679

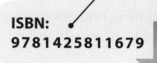

Please note: Some files provided for download have large file sizes. Download times for these larger files will vary based on your download speed.

 ## CONTENTS OF THE DIGITAL RESOURCES

Teacher Resources

- Student Item Analysis
- Practice Page Item Analysis Chart

Student Resources

- Practice Pages
